Whose Resources?

Whose Common Good?

*Towards a New Paradigm
of Environmental Justice and
the National Interest in Indonesia*

Center for International Environment Law (CIEL)

In collaboration with

**HuMa
Perkumpulan untuk Pembaruan Hukum Berbasis
Masyarakat dan Ekologis**
(Association for Community and Ecologically-Based Law Reform)

Lembaga Studi dan Advokasi Masyarakat (ELSAM)
(Institute for Policy Research and Advocacy)

Indonesian Center for Environmental Law (ICEL)

International Centre for Research in Agroforestry (ICRAF)

January 2002

Lynch, Owen J.
     Whose resources? whose common good?: towards
a new paradigm of environmental justice and na-
tional interest in Indonesia / Owen J. Lynch and
Emily Harwell.
Jakarta: Lembaga Studi dan Advokasi Masyarakat
(ELSAM), 2002

     224p. 1,4 cm
     Includes bibliographical references.
     ISBN 979-8981-19-7
     1. Natural resources —legal aspect. 2. Environmen-
     tal Law. I. Whose Resources? Whose Common
     Good? II. Emily Harwell

Anas Priyo
Cover Design

Grammarians. Inc.
Lay Out Design

H. de Foresta (IRD-France) & G. Michon (IRD-France)
Description: Durian (Durio zibethius) season in the
agroforest: a major party for everybody, especially for
children;
Location: Indonesia, West Sumatra Province, Tanah
Datar District, Koto Malintang Village.
Front Cover Photo

LBH Bantaya, Palu, Central Sulawesi
Back Cover Photo

CONTENTS

List of Boxes

ACKNOWLEDGMENTS

Giving proper acknowledgment at the end of a more than five-year collaborative effort is almost impossible. Many people and institutions contributed in large and small ways to this report. Foremost are Sandra Moniaga, Rikardo Simarmata, and Martje Palijama of the Lembaga Studi & Advokasi Masyarakat (ELSAM—the Institute for Policy Research and Advocacy), and now at HuMa, Mas Achmad Santosa, Wiwiek Awiati and Windu Kisworo of the Indonesian Center for Environmental Law (ICEL), Paul "Chip" Fay, Martua Sirait, and Lisken Situmorang of the International Centre for Research in Agroforestry (ICRAF), and the entire staff of BSP KEMALA. Public interest lawyers and law school graduates from throughout Indonesia drafted case studies on legal relationships between the Indonesian state and resource-dependent communities in various regions and they merit special acknowledgment. Their names, organizational affliation, location, and the case studies they drafted are listed below.

Sumatra Region:
- Zulkifli Djaelani—Lembaga Riset dan Advokasi (LRA)/ Institute of Research and Advocacy, Padang.
  Title: "Government's Outlaw Acts toward Indigenous People of Siberut Island."
- Alamsyah Hutabarat—Yayasan Peran/Peran Foundation.
  Title: "Legal Analysis on Forest Fire in Riau Province (A Review)."
- Sofia—Lembaga Riset dan Advokasi/Institute of Research and Advocacy, Tompek Tapian Kandis village, Palembayan, Agam Regency.
  Title: "The Impact of Natural Resource Management on Women's Empowerment."

- Sri Tuti Hariati—Sekretariat Bersama "Pencinta Alam Sumbar", West Sumatra.
  Title: "Legal Conflicts in Mega Mendung Recreational Forest."
- Indra—Menara, Padang.
  Title: "Customary Law Resources of Sungai Pinang Community, Pesisir Selatan."
- Nofitri—Yayasan Bantuan Hukum (YBH) Andalas/Legal Aid Foundation, Andalas.
  Title: "The Livelihood of Traditional Miners in Coal Mining Management in Sawahlunto."

Kalimantan Region:
- Conkordius Kanyan—Lembaga Bela Banua Talino (LBBT)/ Institute of Bela Banua Talino, Pontianak.
  Title: "The Legal Position of Simpang Dyak Tribe's Natural Resource Management in Semandang Kiri Village, Simpang Hulu-Ketapang, West Kalimantan."
- Darius Dalip and Priyana— Human Rights Committee and Institute of Bela Banua Puti Jaji, Samarinda.
  Title: "Indigenous People's Rights in Natural Resource Management in Benung Village, Damai-Kutai, East Kalimantan."
- Tobias Sukanto—Triu Keadilan, Ketapang, West Kalimantan.
  Title: "Indigenous People and Natural Resource Management: Case Study on Traditional Gold Mining of Jungka Tribe in Pondok Natai Village, Tumbang Titi-Ketapang, West Kalimantan."
- Marine Rona—PPSHK–Yayasan Karya Sosial Pancur Kasih/ Community-Based Forestry Management System Empowerment Program of Pancur Kasih Foundation. West Kalimantan.
  Title: "Customary Law as a Legal Option in Forest Resource Management."
- Erma Ranik—Kalimantan Review, Indigenous People Kotif and Entikong (Kotif and entikong village).
  Title: "Policy Analysis on Timber Concession, Utilization and Management and its Impacts on Dayak Communities in West Kalimantan."

- Wahyudi—Lembaga Gemawan/Gemawan Institute, Pemangkat Kota Village, Sambas Regency
  Title: "Marine Resource Management: Between Traditional Wisdom and State Policies: Fishers in Sungai Penuh."
- Abdias Yas—Pancur Kasih, Kenyabur village–Sandai, Ketapang Regency
  Title: "The Struggle of Policy Transformation Towards People's Sovereignty in Natural Resource Management."

Sulawesi Region:
- Matulandi Paat Lontoh Supit—Lembaga Pengkajian dan Pengembangan Sumberdaya/Resource Development and Research Institute, Tomohon.
  Title: "Papakelan Community Defending Their Traditional Forest."
- Jemmy Lumintang—Yayasan Suara Nurani (YSN)/Suara Nurani Foundation, Manado.
  Title: "The Delineation of Bunaken Marine Park and Threats to People and Natural Resources."
- Hedar Laudjeng—Yayasan Bantuan Hukum Bantaya/Bantaya Legal Aid Foundation, Palu.
  Title: "Seeking Space for the Customary Law of Pakava Tribe."
- Sarlan Adi Jaya—Yayasan Suluh/Suluh Foundation, Kendari.
  Title: "Legal and Social Justice Problems in Natural Resource Management: The Case of Moronene Tribe in Laea Hukaea Village within Rawa A'Opa Watumohai."
- Nasrul Jamalludin—Yayasan Bumi Persada/Bumi Persada Foundation.
  Title: "Tenurial Systems and Natural Resource Management in Laalo Tribe in Bangkurung Islets, Banggai."
- Rommy Hiola—Fakultas Kehutanan/School of Forestry, Universitas Bolaang, Mongondow.
  Title: "Forest Resource Tenure and Management in Bogani Nani Wartabone National Park."
- Johny Orah—Yayasan Suara Nurani/Suara Nurani Foundation, Pongolombian village.
  Title: "The Impacts of Geothermal Management on Drinking Water Demand by the Pangolombian Indigenous Community."

Maluku Region:

- Martje Palijama—Lembaga Pengkajian Hukum dan Masyarakat (YLPHM)/Institute of Law and Community Studies, Ambon, Maluku.
  Title: "Mining Exploration Impacts on Haruku Island."
- Stenly Maelissa—Lembaga Pengkajian Hukum dan Masyarakat (YLPHM)/Institute of Law and Community Studies, Ambon, Maluku.
  Title: "The Meaning of Adat Institutions in Natural Resource Preservation Efforts."
- Ferry Sitaniapessy—Baileo Maluku, Ambon.
  Title: "Customary Law Enforcement in Community-Based Resource Management in Nusa Laut Island."

Papua and East Nusa Tenggara Region:

- Edison Robert Giay—Lembaga Pengkajian dan Pemberdayaan Masyarakat Adat/ Institute for Indigenous Community Empowerment and Research, Jayapura, West Papua.
  Title: "The Influences of the Status of Cyclop Nature Reserve on Community-Based Resource Management in North Deponsoro."
- Seprianus Puru Bebe—Yayasan Konsultasi dan Bantuan Hukum Justitia/ Legal Aid and Consultation "Justitia," Kupang, West Timor.
  Title: "Law and Politics, and their Influences on the Rights of Indigenous People of Alas Village, Kobalima-Belu, East Nusa Tenggara."
- Yahya Mabel—Yayasan Bina Adat Wallesi (YBAW)
  Title: "The Importance of the Delineation of Lorentz National Park on Natural Resource Management."
- Frida Kelasin—Lembaga Bantuan Hukum/Legal Aid Institution, Pos Merauke.
  Title: "The Impacts of the Delineation of Wasur National Park on Natural Resource Management."
- Paulus Katamap—Lembaga Pengkajian dan Pemberdayaan Masyarakat Adat (LPPMA)/Institute for Indigenous Community Empowerment and Research, Jayapura, West Papua, Jayapura.

> Title: "Tenurial Systems and Kemtuk Community-Based Forest Management in Kleuku."

- Metuzalak Awom—Lembaga Pendidikan, Pengkajian Pemberdayaan dan Bantuan Hukum Manokwari/Legal Aid, Empowerment, Research and Education Institute.
  Title: "Participatory Critical Legal Analysis with Indigenous People in Arfak Mountains Nature Reserve, Manokwari."
- Oktavianus Mambraku—Yayasan Amkili/Amkili Foundation, Sorong.
  Title: "Empowerment of Moi Indigenous People in Defending their Tenurial Rights over their Forest from the PT Intimura Timber Concession in Sorong."

Java Region:
- Andik Hardiyanto—Lembaga Bantuan Hukum/Legal Aid Institute, Semarang.
  Title: "The Impacts of Natural Resource Allocation Policy: The Case of East Surabaya Coastal Development."

Nationwide:
- Firsty Husbany—Indonesian Center for Environmental Law (ICEL), Jakarta.
  Title: "Legal Concepts of Marine Spatial Planning in Indonesia."
- Myrna Safitri—Program Penelitian dan Pengembangan Antropologi–Ekologi/Anthropological and Ecological Development and Research Program, University of Indonesia, Jakarta.
  Title: "Village, Local Institutions and Forest Resource Management: A Legal Analysis Concerning Village as a Management Unit."

This report goes well beyond the case studies. It aims, among other things, to contribute to the development of policy research, critical analysis, and constructive legal advocacy in the Indonesian context. At the same time, the information and insights contributed by the case study authors were essential in developing and refining the conclusions and recommendations reached in this report. Hopefully, the case study authors and other public interest oriented lawyers and law students will continue to explore, analyze and help develop more equitable and appropriate legal relationships between the local communities and government institutions in Indonesia.

Besides our partners from HuMa, ELSAM, ICEL and ICRAF, many other colleagues took time from busy schedules to review drafts of the report. They include Arthur Blundell, Michael Dove, Noer Fauzi, Mary Melnyk, Steve Rhee, Kathleen Shurcliff, Ronald Titahelu, Frances Seymour, Andy White, Eva Wollenberg, Nonette Royo, Janis Alcorn, Nurina Widagdo, and other anonymous reviewers. Their comments and suggestions were greatly appreciated and enormously helpful.

This book would never have been published without consistent and invaluable help from Shivani Chaudhry and Nina Dwisasanti. In addition, Andre Bald, Matthew Vespa, Carina Bachofen, Enrico Murtula and James Nussbaumer assisted with various research, editing and formatting tasks. Rebecca Lankey, Stacy VanDerWall, and Mellen Candage and Michael Alwan of Grammarians, Inc. likewise provided copy-editing and formatting support that improved the final product. USAID Indonesia—through the auspices of the Biodiversity Support Program's (BSP) KEMALA project—and the Ford Foundation provided most of the funding for this report and the activities that made it possible. Additional support came from the Richard and Rhoda Goldman Fund, and John Street.

On behalf of CIEL and its partners, sincere thanks to all.

Emily E. Harwell and Owen J. Lynch
Center for International Environmental Law
Washington, DC, U.S.A
January 2002

Case Study Locations

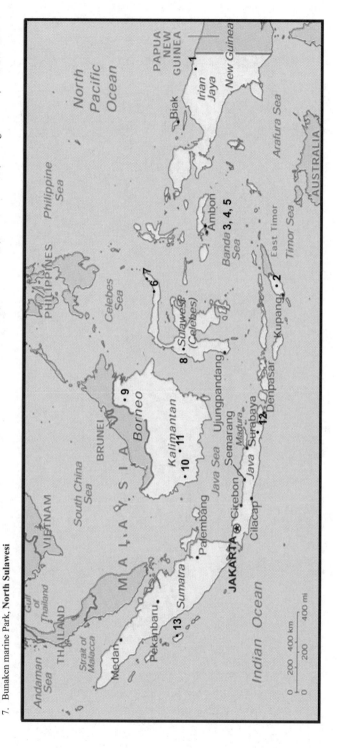

1. Deponsoro Utara, Depapre, Siklop, **Irian Jaya**
2. Alas, Belu, **West Timor**
3. Ihamahu, Paperu, and Siri-Sori, Saparua Island, **Maluku**
4. Nusalaut Island, **Maluku**
5. Haruku Island, **Maluku**
6. Papakelan, Toulimambot, Minahasa, **North Sulawesi**
7. Bunaken marine Park, **North Sulawesi**

8. Tiga Boya, Maravola, Donggala, **Central Sulawesi**
9. Benung, Damai, Kutai, **East Kalimantan**
10. Semandung Kiri, Simpang Hulu, Ketapang, **West Kalimantan**
11. Pondok, Natai, Tumbang Titi, Ketapang, **West Kalimantan**
12. Kedung Cowek, Surabaya, **East Java**
13. Madobak, Siberut Selatan, Mentawai Islands, Padang Pariaman, **West Sumatra**

PREFACE

Recent events in Indonesia are catalyzing important political and legal changes in support of environmental justice. The new Revised Forest Law of 1999 acknowledges that local communities have a key role to play in sustainable forest management. Within the forestry ministry, a new regulation that would authorize the demarcation of indigenous territories within areas designated as state forestland is under review and ongoing revision. The National Land Board, in a related vein, has issued a decree providing for the delineation and registration of community-based *adat* rights in at least some forested areas. In addition, the new National Human Rights Law contains specific recognition of the government's responsibility to recognize and protect the differences, needs, and cultural identity of indigenous peoples. This law explicitly calls for recognition of "community-made land rights," which this report refers to as community-based property rights (CBPRs).

These new policies reflect the democratic spirit that has been developing in Indonesia since the fall of President Suharto and his New Order regime in May 1998. The emerging political will that is prompting the development of new policies is partly due to the growing influence of Indonesian civil society. Examples of important new civil society initiatives abound. They include the Forum Komunikasi Kehutanan Masyarakat (Communications Forum on Community Forestry/FKKM) national seminar on forestry reform in June 1998 and the Congress of Indigenous Peoples of the Archipelago, which was held in March 1999 and was cosponsored by an impressive array of Indonesian non-governmental organizations (NGOs), and resulted in the formation of the Indigenous Peoples' Association of the Archipelago (AMAN). These and other civil society initiatives, including an impressive array of community-based efforts, are helping to lay the foundation for new national laws and policies that support sustainable community-based natural resource management.

Many challenges, however, still remain. Amendments in August 2000 to the 1945 Constitution need to be interpreted and implemented. Long-standing reliance on the New Order reinterpretation of Article 33 of the founding document needs be challenged and reconsidered. The 1999 Revised Forest Law requires implementation mechanisms for ensuring meaningful community involvement in forest management, including timber harvesting. The newly created Ministry of Marine Affairs has yet to define its jurisdictional mandate, including its role in and strategies for promoting community-based initiatives. The legal mechanisms for implementing new laws on decentralization of natural resource management remain unclear, as does the extent to which local communities will be involved.

These challenges highlight the urgent need in Indonesia to design and implement creative efforts and solutions that balance prevailing national legal tendencies by giving greater emphasis to needs and contributions of indigenous and other rural peoples, particularly those pertaining to local incentives for conservation and sustainable development. This is especially important where local people are directly dependent on important and threatened environmental resources such as forests, rangelands, marine and coastal areas, and where they possess local knowledge about how to manage those resources sustainably.

The Center for International Environmental Law (CIEL) is a public interest environmental law organization based in Washington, DC, United States. CIEL is part of a growing movement and informal network of civil society institutions from various parts of the world that are committed to promoting sustainable development and the public interest.

CIEL has been working closely with three leading Jakarta-based public interest law organizations that focus on the connections between national and local legal environmental issues. The Perkumpulan untuk Pembaruan Hukum Berbasis Masyarakat dan Ekologis (HuMa, Association for Community and Ecologically Based Law Reform), Lembaga Studi and Advokasi Masyarakat (ELSAM, Institute for Policy Research and Advocacy) and the Indonesian Center for Environmental Law (ICEL) have been collaborating with CIEL during the research and writing phase of this report (1997 to 2001). ELSAM and CIEL supported public interest lawyers and recent law school graduates from throughout Indonesia as they conducted case studies on the legal relationships between local communities and the Indonesian state. ICEL and CIEL collaboratively have been monitoring developments in national laws and policies concerning natural resources since 1997. CIEL has also worked with the International Centre for Research in Agroforestry (ICRAF) in Bogor, which has been at the forefront of examining and developing policies that would provide local communities security of access and management to land and resources in a way that promotes both justice and environmental protection.

This report is a product of this intensive, ongoing collaborative effort. Being in charge of drafting and editing, CIEL is solely responsible for any errors and omissions. CIEL hopes that the report provides a substantive, useful, and enduring contribution to efforts to promote environmental justice and sustainable development in Indonesia.

David Hunter
Executive Director
Center for International Environmental Law

Acronyms

Acronym	Bahasa Indonesia	English
AMAN	Aliansi Masyarakat Adat Nusantara	Alliance of Indigenous Communities of the Archipelago
BATB	Berita Acara Tata Batas	Forestland Delineation Official Report
BPN	Badan Pertanahan National	National Land Board
CBNRM	Pengelolaan Sumber Daya Alam Berbasis Masyarakat (PSDABM)	Community-Based Natural Resource Management
CBPRs	Hak Kepemilikan Berbasis Masyarakat	Community-Based Property Rights
DDTK	Desa Dengan Tujuan Konservasi	Designated Conservation Village
DPR	Dewan Perwakilan Rakyat	National House of Representatives
DPR-D	Dewan Perwakilan Rakyat Daerah	Regional Parliament
ELSAM	Lembaga Studi dan Advokasi Masyarakat	Institute for Policy Research and Advocacy (NGO)
FKKM	Forum Komunikasi Kehutanan Masyarakat	Community Forestry Communication Forum

Acronym	Bahasa Indonesia	English
FECRC	Komite Reformasi Kehutanan dan Perkebunan (KRKP)	Forestry and Estate Crops Reform Committee
GBHN	Garis-Garis Besar Haluan Negara	National Legal Guidelines
GOLKAR	Golangan Karya	Former Ruling Party (based on social "functional groups")
HKM	Hutan Kemasyarakatan	(State Organized) Community Forest
HPH	Hak Pengusahaan Hutan	Timber Concession
HPHH	Hak Pengusahaan Hasil Hutan	Forest Products Concession
HR	Hutan Rakyat	Community Forest
ICRAF	—	International Centre for Research in Agroforestry (NGO)
IPRA	—	Indigenous Peoples' Rights Act (Philippines)
KUDETA	Koalisi untuk Demokratisasi Sumberdaya Alam	Coalition for the Democratization of Natural Resources
KAPET	Kawasan Pembangunan Ekonomi Terpadu	Designated Integrated Economic Development Zone
KDTI/K	Kawasan Daerah Dengan Tujuan Istemewa/Khusus	Special Use Area
KTSW	Kelompok Toga Sumber Waras	Sumber Waras family health self-reliance club

Acronym	Bahasa Indonesia	English
LATIN	Lembaga Alam Tropika Indonesia	Institute for Indonesian Tropical Resources (NGO)
LMD	Lembaga Musyawarah Desa	Village Consultative Body
LBBT	Lembaga Bela Banua Talino	Legal Aid Council (NGO)
MPR	Majelis Permusyawarahan Rakyat	People's Consultative Assembly
Pemda	Pemerintah Daerah	Regional Government
Perda	Peraturan Daerah	Regional Government Regulation
Permen	Peraturan Mentri	Ministerial Regulation
PETI	Pertambangan Tanpa Ijin	illegal mining
PIR	pola inti rakyat	smallholder nucleus estate
PLN	Perusahaan Listrik Negara	National Power Corporation
PP	Peraturan Pemerintah	Government Regulation
PPSDAK	Pemberdayaan Pengelolaan Sumber Daya Alam Kerakyatan	Community Resource Management Empowerment (NGO)
Propenas	Program Pembangunan Nasional	Five Year Plan
PT	Perseroan Terbatas	Limited Liability Company
SK	Surat Keputusan	Ministerial Regulation
Tap MPR	Ketetapan Musyawarah Perwakilan Rakyat	Decree of the People's Consultative Assembly
TGHK	Tata Guna Hutan Kesepakatan	Consensus Forest Use Planning

Acronym	Bahasa Indonesia	English
UU	Undang-Undang	National Law
UUD	Undang-Undang Dasar	Indonesian Constitution 1945
UUPK	Undang-Undang Pokok Kehutanan	Basic Forestry Law 1967 (BFL)
VOC	Vereenigde Oost-Indische Compagnie (Dutch)	Netherlands East Indies Company
WALHI	Wahana Lingkungan Hidup Indonesia	Indonesia Environmental Forum/Friends of the Earth–Indonesia

GLOSSARY

BAHASA INDONESIA

Adat	Customary (community-based) laws, practices and institutions
Desa	(Administrative) Village
Bupati	District Government Head
Camat	Sub-district Government Head
Hutan Adat	Customary Forest
Forum Pemerhati Kehutanan	Forest Watch Program
Pancasila	The Five Principles, which constitute the founding ideology of the Indonesian state: belief in one God, national unity, humanitarianism, people's sovereignty, social justice, and prosperity
Wilayah Adat	Adat Management Area
Kopermas	Community Cooperatives
O'o ukul	Elders of the Confederation
Meadati Buah	Customary Practice Ensuring Principles of Ecological Balance

ENGLISH

Legal personality	State-recognized legal entity such as a corporation or cooperative

INTRODUCTION:
NATURAL RESOURCES AND INDONESIA'S BUDDING DEMOCRACY

Indonesia faces the most dramatic opportunity for altering the futures of its people and its philosophy of governance since it declared independence in 1945. In casting off thirty-two years of repressive authoritarian government and corruption in 1998, Indonesia's leaders publicly committed to return to the constitutional principles of popular sovereignty, social justice, and humanitarianism. Fundamental changes in policy and governance are popularly desired and urgently needed. When she was a leader of the opposition to Suharto's New Order, Megawati Sukarnoputri acknowledged as much by committing herself and her administration to democratic reform. In her words, "the essence of democracy as a way of life is respect for other people, respect for human beings. Thus the struggle of transforming our society into a democracy is basically the struggle of persuading ourselves to be respectful towards others in our daily lives. Unless we succeed in fostering genuine respect toward others, democracy will remain an empty jargon in our society" (Sukarnoputri 1997).

Although the new government of President Sukarnoputri is still taking shape as this report goes to press in January 2002, the initial exuberance over the possibilities of *reformasi* (reform) after the fall of the Suharto dictatorship in May 1998 has largely ebbed. Meanwhile, the hard work of reconstructing the nation continues. Throughout Indonesia, fundamental concepts of national philosophy and state administration and functions are being challenged and reinvented. Legal control of Indonesia's natural resources is at the center of many of these fundamental debates, and the outcomes will have broad and enduring impacts.

Indonesia is home to some of the world's most valuable natural resources. It is one of the most biodiverse countries in the world

(Mittermeier et al. 1997) and one of the nine most economically and environmentally important countries (Flavin 2001). Its natural resources are vital to Indonesia's government, its citizens and to the international community. As with elsewhere around the globe, linkages between natural resource management, democratization and human rights have become increasingly apparent in Indonesia. The national economy relies on resource extraction,[1] and resource-dependent rural communities comprise 60% of the population.[2] The challenge for law and policy makers is to think creatively about how to best address past abuses and promote more democratic and sustainable resource management in the future. Without democratic reforms and a return to public confidence in government, reconciliation and stability in Indonesia are likely to remain elusive.

This report explores issues that must be addressed if Indonesia's natural resource sector is to be substantively democratized, a development that would also contribute to establishing necessary conditions for conservation and sustainable development. The report focuses on the failure of current policy and legal approaches and attempts to articulate a new paradigm that emphasizes local community well-being as an integral and important part of the national interest and Indonesia's constitutional mandates. Unlike prior approaches, this new paradigm would not allow those who benefit least from natural resource extraction to also bear the greatest costs.

A reasoned reinterpretation of Indonesia's constitution recognizes and protects indigenous community-based property rights (CBPRs) and systems of governance. These provisions have been obscured by broad claims of state authority to control natural resources and village governance, ostensibly for the national interest. Article 18 implicitly guarantees legal entitlement by local people to participate meaningfully in managing natural resources they directly rely on for their lives and livelihoods. As such, the ongoing unconstitutional failure of the Indonesian Republic to recognize community-based *adat* property rights must end, and past crimes in which community resources were seized without due process must be rectified.

A move toward environmental justice in Indonesia's natural resource laws and policies will require the creation of new formal management arrangements that ensure meaningful involvement by natural resource-dependent groups (including indigenous, mixed, and non-indigenous peoples) and more equitable distribution of resource benefits. New laws based on old assumptions will not adequately alter the present unsustainable course. A move toward an environmental justice paradigm requires legal reform and repeal, as well as more democratic interpretations of existing laws.

Old States, Old Assumptions

National legislation regulating both village governance and natural resource is still based on the primacy of centralized state authority as the ultimate arbiter of "national good." Recent decentralization initiatives have not fundamentally altered this enduring fact; rather they involve the devolution of some state powers to more local governments. Especially during the New Order regime, concepts involving local community-based rights were pitted against ideas about modernity and the national interest. This state-based paradigm reached its pinnacle in the early 1980s when the New Order state classified over 75% of the total land area as State Forest, including over 90% of the Outer Islands. The approach ignored pre-existing local rights to millions of hectares of land, forests, coastlines and other natural resources. In what can be considered as the largest land seizure in history (Fay and Sirait 2001), the state claimed authority as the only legitimate manager of all resources in these areas and has used this authority to prioritize economic development, usually at the expense and interests of local communities.

Since Dutch colonization, the state has asserted itself as the ultimate source of law, rights, and order, claiming a monopoly on authority and governance. This assertion of state authority, which was especially unaccountable during President Suharto's thirty-two-year campaign for economic development, contributed to the rapid depletion of Indonesia's natural resources, usually to the detriment of resource-dependent communities. Recent estimates put annual deforestation at 1.7 million hectares (World Bank 2000a) and predict that if current conditions persist, lowland forests in Sumatra will be destroyed by 2005, and in Kalimantan by 2010 (Holmes 2000). Widespread resentment over state expropriation of community-based rights and the narrow flow of resource benefits to a few elites has fueled violence throughout the archipelago (see Chapter III). The widespread nature of these remarkably similar conflicts demonstrates that these are not isolated cases. Rather, they provide compelling evidence of the devastating impacts that national legislation has had on Indonesia's rural resource users and of the rapaciousness of national elites and their international partners.

The imposition of central state authority over resource control and village governance is founded on false assumptions about the character of the local people, their institutions, and the value of nature itself. These misperceptions persist because they facilitate the expropriation of traditional community-based land rights and the introduction of more "productive" or more "modern" uses, such as timber extraction, mining, commercial fishing, or plantation agriculture—a situation that Dove (1983) has called "a political economy of ignorance" (see also Scott 1999).

The first of these misperceptions is the persistent negative stereotype of rural people that still permeates state policies. Local people are assumed to be *absent* from valuable natural resource landscapes (Lynch 1990).[3] Plans are made and maps drawn as if these landscapes are unpopulated and unclaimed. If local people somehow come into the field of view of state resource planners, they are assumed, regardless of ecological or cultural contexts, to be undifferentiated *destroyers* of nature who must be removed to protect natural resource.[4] Further, local people are assumed to be *illegal* occupants and labeled "squatters" or "poachers." This de-legitimizes their participation, including that of local people who have lived in and managed their natural landscapes for generations.

Second, although many local communities have long had their own governing institutions, which are explicitly recognized by Article 18 of Indonesia's constitution, the view of village government as incapable and in need of state "guidance" has pervaded national legislation since the New Order (see Chapter II). Throughout Suharto's New Order regime (1965–1998), the populace was regarded by the state as a "floating mass" dangerously vulnerable to manipulation by political opposition.[5] The New Order state strove to curtail community-based control over village affairs, ostensibly to achieve national developmental goals. The legal pluralism celebrated by Article 18 was seen by the New Order state administratively inefficient and a hindrance to development.

Finally, the value of natural resources is still narrowly defined under state legislation as being purely economic, with common assets to be exploited in ways that advance the national economy.

This view not only repudiates local communities' property rights, but also precludes identifying alternative values for natural resources. The economic development paradigm that fosters this narrow view of resource value also conflates "national interest" with local benefit by assuming that developing the national economy will produce prosperity for all citizens. Yet policies that diminish local community rights and management while advocating economic development have failed to deliver equitable development. Some estimates have calculated that over 80 million people, or 40% of the population, lived below the poverty line in 1999 (ILO 2000).[6] This same policy environment fostered epidemic corruption in the New Order government, which further exacerbated resource degradation, land expropriation, and local poverty. The prevailing official state subsidized patterns of resource use are in clear contradiction of the Indonesian Constitution, as well as several basic resource laws, that mandate the state support for the sustainable use of natural resources so as to improve the welfare of all of Indonesian citizens.[7]

Indonesia's government ministers themselves readily admit the state's failure to sustainably manage natural resources within its borders[8] and have publicly voiced their commitment to reconcile past injustices by the state.[9] Unfortunately, legislation to accomplish democratic resource management has been slow to emerge. In this legislative vacuum, local contests over resources are already unfolding in ad hoc fashion, often without firm direction or legal mechanisms. As the political futures of Indonesia's elites and their international allies become ever more uncertain, the cost of staying in power increases. This ensures that control over Indonesia's rich resources will continue to play a central role in cash-strapped local, regional, and national politics.

Summary of the Report

Indonesia's social and ecological futures are laden with challenges. The claims on Indonesia's natural resources are multiple and contested, complicated by dynamic and fractured political and economic agendas, complex and shifting identities, local community mobility (both forced and voluntary), and so on. This report makes no claim that all local communities are capable managers of all natural resources located within their domains. Rather, it argues that democracy and environmental justice require that local people have a voice in official decision making processes that directly affect their lives and livelihoods.

The case studies and other research highlighted in this report do not suggest a universal response. Instead, experience demonstrates that multiple arrangements are needed to address different contexts, communities, and resources. What is clear is that transparent and accountable mechanisms of decision-making, dispute management, monitoring, and enforcement are essential to the democratization of natural resource management.

These are complex and weighty questions, and the stakes are obviously high. Some political actors struggling for power continue to incite discontent and violence for personal gain. As is already evident from events in East and West Timor, Ambon and Northern Maluku, Aceh, and Kalimantan, following the overthrow of the Suharto regime, substantive change is neither quick nor without conflict. Careful groundwork for good governance, based upon successful experiences at the local level, must be established for changes to endure.

The report begins by describing a brief history of the origins of the state-based paradigm of natural resource management. It documents the inherent tensions since Indonesia's political independence of recognizing legal and institutional diversity and enforcing village uniformity as a means to control local governance and resources. Case studies are used to present and highlight the implications and impacts of this legal history on local ecological and social landscapes. The case studies and other research relied on in this report also highlight the impacts of state laws and policies on local conflicts and community leadership, including the management of institutions and property rights. They show that conflicts stem from divergent perceptions of authority and the value of resources and from systemic flaws in the implementation of progressive constitutional provisions and laws.

Next, the report turns to the recent developments in democratization of resource management since the end of Suharto's reign in 1998. Important new laws and regulations are introduced and examined and progressive provisions in some old laws and policies are reexamined. Recent developments within the Ministry of Forestry and Estate Crops, the largest government bureaucracy with the largest degree of legal jurisdiction over natural resources in Indonesia, are reviewed and commented on. Lastly the report closes with a reexamination of the prevailing concept regarding Indonesia's national interest; it offers a broader and more inclusive concept in light of current constitutional and legislative provisions. Recommendations on ways to design more democratic and just arrangements in order to increase participation of and support by local communities in natural resource management are also provided.

Ultimately, this report manifests hope for and belief in Indonesia and its people. New ways of thinking and addressing natural resource rights and conflicts are needed in Indonesia, as well as many other nations. President Sukarnoputri observed in 1997 before she assumed office, "Laws are created not out of the interest to protect people, but out of the different kind of interests which in many cases have nothing to do with people" (Sukarnoputri 1997). Her views have not changed since. This report was written in support of ongoing efforts throughout Indonesia to change this trajectory and democratize laws so that they reflect the interest of all of Indonesia's people. Only time will tell if these efforts are successful.

Notes

1. Curtis Runyan of WorldWatch reports that "under Sukarno, the export of raw materials had been nearly non-existent. But by 1970, about 60% of Indonesia's GDP came from extracting and exporting natural resources.... Since the 1990s, manufacturing and other sectors have made large inroads, but resource extraction's share of the GDP remains around 40%—still a significant share. In addition, the absolute value of resources extracted annually in the 1990s has more than doubled the value extracted in 1970." (Worldwatch Magazine, June 1998).

2. World Bank 1999 and Indonesia's Bureau of Statistics (BPS) 1998 figures put the percentage of rural population in Indonesia at 65%.

3. While government (Ministry of Forestry) statistics consistently overlooked or underestimated the number of forest communities (in 1985 official government estimates put the number of forest dependent people at 1.2 million (Harahap 1991, 3)), Lynch (1990) estimated forest dwelling communities in Indonesia a decade ago to be over 65 million. Such high numbers should not lead to a simplistic assumption of impact on land or forest cover. Elucidation of such a relationship requires an analysis of

particular natural resource management practices. Further, Malthusian assumptions about the correlation between population and resource degradation typically overlook impacts from such factors as priority access by industrial resource extraction enterprise and increasing demands from national and international urban centers for agricultural, fuel, timber, and other resource products, as well as real estate development, including golf and resort facilities (Lynch and Talbott 15–17, 1995).

4. Contrary to this prevailing stereotype, which is reflected in national laws throughout the world, including Indonesia's, a recently prepared map by WWF shows a significant overlap of the world's richest areas of biodiversity and ancient forests with high concentrations of indigenous cultures. See www.panda.org/resources/publications/sustainability/indigenous3.

5. Law No. 3/1975 forbids the organization of political parties at the village level.

6. The International Labor Organization (ILO) followed the Indonesian Bureau of Statistics definition of poor people as those who cannot afford food with a nutritional value of 2,000 calories a day, or per capita earnings of less than 52,000 rupiah (about US$3.50) a month in urban areas and 41,000 rupiahs (about US$2.70) in rural areas. The World Bank's World Development Indicators report for 1998 estimated the percentage of population below the poverty line to be 20% but did not specify how this figure was calculated. Indonesian economist Faisal Basri calculates that 82% of Indonesians live on US$30 per month or less (Eyal Press, "The Soeharto Lobby," The Progressive, May 1997).

7. 1945 Constitution, Article 33, Section 3; Basic Forestry Law, Considerations; Basic Law on Conservation of Biological Diversity and Ecosystems, Considerations, Article 3, Article 7; Basic Agrarian Law; Basic Mining Law.

8. The Indonesian Forestry Minister himself admitted publicly that the deforestation rate over the last five years has been 1.6 million ha annually (Mahmudi 2001), which he blamed on "inappropriate land management, illegal logging, swidden agriculture, large scale forest clearing, forest fires and economic crisis." In response the Department made a twelve-point public commitment to the CGI (Consultative Group on Indonesia), which advises the International Monetary Fund (IMF).

9. President Abudurahman Wahid's opening comments at the National Conference on Natural Resources, Jakarta on May 23, 2000. See Chapter V for more on these remarks.

I.

COMMUNITY-BASED PROPERTY RIGHTS: A CONCEPTUAL NOTE

Property rights, as is well recognized, are an important factor in natural resource management (Bromley 1998, 2000; McCay and Acheson 1990). Yet terms and concepts concerning property rights have deeply imbedded and often different meanings for different people. As efforts to understand the relationships between different domains of work and scholarship increase, new insights concerning challenges posed by language are emerging. The emphasis given by "poststructuralists" to language and interpretation is having an enormous impact upon thinking and scholarship in the liberal arts and social sciences, including theories and concepts related to property rights.

When scholars and policy-makers seek to understand and describe relationships between one field of thought and another, they build bridges between different forms of expertise and different constituencies. Yet, it is increasingly evident that such crossing of disciplines also produces disparities and misunderstandings between the language and concepts developed in one line of work and the language and concepts developed in another. Normal habits of human thought, meanwhile, often still lead people to believe that language is a neutral medium, simply a way of pointing to objects and concepts we all recognize and understand. Yet it is increasingly evident that language often poses big problems when information is shared between different sectors of study and action.[1]

These problems are evident in discussions about property rights. Different concepts of property lend support to and are consequently reproduced by particular political-economic or cultural orientations.[2]

1

As such, it is especially important to define how the term "community-based property rights" (CBPRs) is used and understood in this report.

The Law and Communities Program of the Center for International Environmental Law (CIEL) coined the acronym "CBPRs" in 2000, although the term was already being used in the mid 1990s. Among other things, the CBPR concept is purposefully designed to be useful in advocating on behalf of local communities and helping them protect their rights to manage and control natural resources. It is the product of a program objective to develop and promote applied legal concepts that are more pro-community and more equitable than widely used terms such as common property and "community-based natural resource management," which is also known by the acronym (CBNRM). The concept of CBPRs provides an intentional and strategic conceptual contrast to CBNRM, common property, and other terms such as co-management, joint management, etc.

As discussed in this chapter, legal recognition of CBPRs by governments should be understood to be an aspirational and optimal goal for many local communities that are or will be negotiating natural resource management agreements with government. Although full legal recognition of CBPRs as private may not be the final outcome of a particular negotiation with states such as Indonesia that claim ownership and control over vast areas, it is important that long-marginalized local communities and advocates on their behalf know of and pursue an optimal ideal outcome. This is fundamental to any credible and fair negotiation process involving rural peoples and their property rights.[3]

Meanwhile, over the past two decades, many donor institutions and governments (although by no means all) have increasingly supported CBNRM-type initiatives, and this is generally a positive development. Most CBNRM policies and programs, however, are still limited in scope and are predicated on an assumption of state ownership of land and other natural resources. As such, the state typically retains primary management authority and merely grants legal rights (or legal "privileges" as in the case of India) to local communities to use and benefit from certain natural resources in a defined area in return for local communities agreeing to assume certain duties. Indeed, CBNRM is commonly (mis)understood to refer to formal government programs rather than to local community practices.

Defining Community-Based Property Rights

In this report, property rights are not considered to necessarily or always be contingent on state grants or formal documentation.[4] Like human rights, which derive their authority from and are recognized by international law as well as by natural law concepts, the existence of CBPRs is not necessarily dependent on government or any assumption of state creation, grant or recognition. Rather, CBPRs encompass ubiquitous and very real local-level dynamics in which many rural people establish, maintain and enforce community-based management rights and obligations regarding natural resource use and development. Typically, longer-established communities, and especially indigenous ones, have more developed understandings of and reliance on their CBPRs, many of which have been formed in response to local environmental conditions.[5]

Community-based property rights *by definition* emanate from and are enforced by communities. The *distinguishing feature* of CBPRs is that they derive their authority from the community in which they operate, not from the nation-state where they are located. Formal legal recognition or grant of CBPRs by the state, however, is generally desirable and can help to ensure that CBPRs are respected and used in pursuit of the public interest.[6]

References to community-based natural resource management and property rights should be used only with regard to initiatives that are primarily controlled and authorized from within a community. Externally initiated activities with varying degrees of community participation should not be referred to as community-based, at least not until the community exercises primary decision-making authority. Unfortunately, the term "community-based" is loosely used and applied too often to initiatives with only the limited involvement and support of local communities.

By contrast with widely used and largely uniform Western concepts, CBPRs within a given local community typically encompass a complex, and often overlapping, bundle of rights that are understood and respected by a self-defined group of local people. Rights in the bundle can be grouped in various ways. One way is to identify six categories that encompass rights of: (1) use, (2) control, (3) indirect economic gain, and (4) transfer, as well as, (5) residual and (6) symbolic rights.[7]

CBPRs are not equivalent or even similar to "open access" regimes. By definition, open access indicates the absence of any management rules or authority. Unlike with common property, open access situations are by definition non-exclusionary.

CBPRs often include, but are not limited to, common property. They can also encompass various kinds of individual rights and kinship rights, such as inherited rights to agricultural fields and fallows, gardens, planted or tended trees or rattan clusters, and the like. CBPRs likewise can include rights to land, wildlife, water, forest products, fish, marine products, intellectual property, and so forth. CBPRs may vary in time and place to include rights to seasonally available resources such as fruit, game, fish, water, or grazing areas. They often specify under what circumstances and to what extent certain resources are available to individuals and communities to inhabit, to harvest, to hunt and gather on, and to inherit.

CBPRs are similar to, but not the same as, collective rights. The concept of CBPRs as used in this report is more specific and defined than the notion of collective rights. CBPRs specifically refer to legal rights that derive their legitimacy from the communities themselves and not the nation states where they are located. This emphasis is not semantic; it is intended to highlight the multiple sources and characteristics of CBPRs and how they translate into practice. Some CBPRs are collective, but not all collective rights are CBPRs.[8]

The concept of "collective rights" is not limited to natural resources and property rights; it refers more broadly to any rights held by a group of people. While the term "collective rights" has been used in Latin America to refer to the territorial rights of indigenous peoples, it has many other applications. The legal rights of a nation state over land and other natural resources and the rights of corporations to their financial assets, for example, can also be referred to as "collective rights." Even in the realm of indigenous peoples' rights, collective rights do not necessarily refer only to a group's ownership and use of natural resources.

Throughout Indonesia and much of the majority (developing) world, community-based property rights exist in many places and are often distinguishable from Western property rights concepts. Western concepts are based largely on state-created and protected private individual rights, or on socialist concepts that theoretically vest the state with ownership of all land and other natural resources in order to supposedly best promote the public interest.

CBPRs or community-based tenure systems? It could be argued that to limit confusion with Western concepts it would be best to use the term "tenure systems" instead of the term property rights. The fear is that any widespread application of the term "property rights" to indigenous rights, even if prefaced by the term community-based, could weaken and undermine traditional local control of natural resources. This concern is largely based on the widespread and increasing commodification of property rights throughout the world and the fear that legal recognition of CBPRs would be a prelude to their sale.

It merits emphasizing that the CBPR concept is meant primarily for external use, i.e., to communicate to outsiders that a local community owns its natural resources and exercises primary management authority over them. To be most effective, this requires use of the term property rights, precisely because of the importance of communicating to governments and other external actors exactly what local communities possess. Most advocates for local communities are very concerned about the market and the alienation of community-based property rights. But they are also concerned about the oftentimes more immediate prospect of government and private sector interests asserting superior rights and arbitrarily overriding local community-based tenure systems.

Widespread reliance on the term tenure, and not property rights, can make usurpation by outsiders easier. However more accommodating to local variation the use of sociological terms over legal terms may be, they also provide more powerful external actors with strategic ambiguity that can be exploited against vulnerable local communities unfamiliar with dominant legal concepts.

Furthermore, unlike individual property rights, legally recognized CBPRs would not be as prone to commodification as they are group-held, and decisions to sell any rights must involve the group.[9] Legal recognition of private CBPRs would not necessarily preclude the eventual disaggregation of individual property rights if a particular local community wanted to do this. It would, however, provide at least a temporary restraint on alienation, thereby giving community members more time to adjust to market pressures.

In sum, use of the term property rights makes clear to the state and other dominant external forces—in language they understand and rely on—exactly what a particular local community asserts its rights to be and aspires to get legally recognized by the state. Besides fostering clarity and limiting misunderstandings, use of common language can help limit opportunities for collusion and manipulation by outsiders. An analogous situation involves participatory community mapping. The concept of maps is not indigenous in most areas of Indonesia covered by *adat* CBPRs. Initially, mapping was opposed by some local community leaders and field-based social scientists as portraying perimeter boundaries in ways and locations that were not reflective of indigenous ideas and customs. But an increasing number of indigenous communities are mapping their ancestral territories in Indonesia and elsewhere. These maps have already proven in some instances to be valuable weapons of the weak in resisting state-sanctioned encroachment and usurpation. See, for example, Chapin and Threlkeld (2001); Alcorn and Royo (2000); Bennagen et al. (2000).

Decentralization and Community-Based Property Rights

The concept of CBPRs relied on in this report is comprehensive and flexible. It is also markedly distinct from decentralization initiatives currently underway in Indonesia and elsewhere. Decentralization can help foster and support legal recognition of CBPRs and various types of CBNRM initiatives, but decentralization to local government units does not necessarily lead to such outcomes. In some countries, decentralization/devolution can even preclude them, and purposely so, as local government officials assume and maintain legal control of valuable resources to fund local government costs.

As this report shows, throughout Indonesia there are literally tens of thousands of local leaders and their constituencies outside of formal local government units. Indonesia's now-empowered *kabupaten* (district) governments typically encompass vast areas that include many local (indigenous/migrant) communities. Despite official Indonesian emphasis on village uniformity, traditional villages, local communities, and CBPRs are heterogeneous and dynamic. And many local communities and CBPRs in Indonesia exist and function outside of official government structures.

One symbolically important and practical conceptual tool for clarifying these facts is to distinguish between the *grant of legal rights* by the state and the *legal recognition of CBPRs*. As already noted, legal rights do not emanate solely from the government of Indonesia or from other nation-states. There are various theories of law and jurisprudence that acknowledge as much.[10] When national governments own land and other natural resources, they often decentralize authority to local government units or local officials, which then in some instances grant management/property rights to local communities located within their jurisdiction. But when community-based property rights already cover an area, the state may (and often should) be obliged to recognize these rights, especially when the area is an ancestral domain/indigenous territory that pre-exists the post-colonial state and its assertions of ownership.

Legal Recognition of Community-Based Property Rights

Government recognition of CBPRs, especially indigenous ones, is often desirable and necessary. But it need not always entail formal codification or the issuance of any specific documents. More important is the government's fulfillment of its responsibility to help resource-dependent communities defend and benefit from sustainably managed natural resources, whether public or private. In many instances, the best way for governments to promote environmental justice, including local incentives for conservation and sustainable management, would be to recognize existing community-based property rights wherever supported by locally appropriate forms of evidence such as farm fallows, orchards, gravesites, and so forth.[11] As an initial step, this can be accomplished by creating a legal presumption of local community ownership wherever such evidence exists.[12]

There are many reasons for legally recognizing CBPRs. First and foremost, in Indonesia and many other countries the constitution can be interpreted as already protecting the CBPRs of indigenous peoples (i.e., original long-term occupants). Legally recognizing these rights would be a positive and crucial step toward ensuring that the constitution is invoked to protect and promote the well-being of all of Indonesia's citizens. In many countries where conflict is epidemic, the legal recognition—or in some instances the legal grant—of community-based rights would also contribute to goodwill between local communities and governments.

Legal recognition of CBPRs provides state assurance that local people will be better able to profit from investments of their time and labor. It would provide local communities with state-sanctioned authority to prevent migration into their territories, which often overlaps with protected areas and other fragile ecosystems rich in biodiversity. It would likewise help local communities better protect and maintain natural resources by bolstering the enforcement of local management regulations.

Property rights, of course, by themselves do not provide adequate incentives and conditions for sustainable management; they are a necessary, but insufficient, condition. They need to be complemented with technical assistance and other forms of help to develop and strengthen local organizational capacities and to support sustainable management and conservation, along with appropriate credit programs that provide economic alternatives to the sale or overextraction of resources.

Rethinking Property Rights

As already indicated, an important strategy for using law to promote better and more just environmental governance involves rethinking prevailing theories of property rights in ways that can be constructively applied to benefit local peoples and institutions. Most property rights theorists and students still rely on a four-part typology of property: private (which is a misnomer because it actually means individual), commons, state, and open access (the last term referring to a situation where no defined property rights exist). This typology has been useful in distinguishing common property from open access (Ostrom 1991; Bromley 1992). It has also been perhaps the most important component of ongoing efforts to challenge the impacts of Garret Hardin's influential article, "The Tragedy of the Commons" (Hardin 1968), which is actually about the tragedy of "open access" and not any tragedy of "the commons."[13]

The continued and largely uncritical reliance on this four-part typology hampers the development of effective legal and policy tools for helping local people gain recognition of their CBPRs. The prevailing typology simply does not work well in law and policy-making or in project design processes. It overlooks the spatially and temporally dynamic nature of CBPR systems. It also promotes the abrupt and often arbitrary disaggregation of individual rights from the community-based systems in which they exist and are legitimated. The World Bank and most other financial lending institutions, as well as most nation-states, promote this disaggregation in the belief that individual property rights are superior to group-based rights as they can be bought and sold—that is, marketed more easily—and this is understood to enhance productivity, which is true in many instances with regard to arable land. At the same time, the prevailing approach overlooks important ecological, cultural, and equity considerations and undermines existing CBPRs, including common property.

Another problem with the prevailing four-part typology is that it implies that there is always a distinct and separable commons within CBPR regimes. It is almost impossible, however, to isolate "the commons" within a CBPR system with any precision. There are usually many different, and often overlapping, types of commons within a CBPR system. Neighboring villages often share access to natural resources, and sub-groups within a community may limit access of other community members to an orchard or a fallow field. As such, more practical and applied ways to think about property concepts and rights are needed.

Spectrum of Property Rights

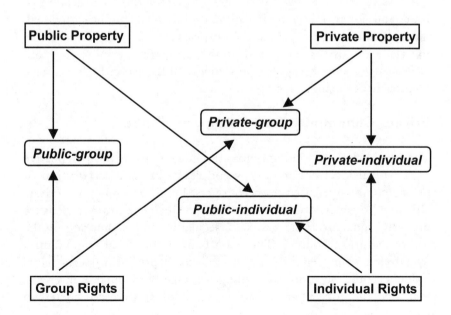

One approach would be to think in terms of two conceptual and interrelated spectra. The first spectrum has public property on one end and private property on the other. "Public" means it is owned by the state, and "private" means that it is not owned by the state. However, the degrees of private and public ownership can vary, with some private rights being heavily encumbered by state conditionalities such as easements and zoning restrictions and some public rights being largely unregulated. Private titles, therefore, are not necessarily always the strongest type of property right, although generally they are. It depends on what is in the bundle of property rights. To know what a specific property right entails, whether it is a private title or a public lease, ultimately requires that the bundle be deconstructed and defined.[14]

The other spectrum has individual rights on one end and group rights on the other. The group end basically refers to CBPR regimes, most of which typically include individual rights as well as common properties.[15] As previously stated, the fundamental characteristic of CBPRs is that their primary legitimacy is drawn from the community in which they exist, not from the nation-state in which they are located. The concept of CBPRs is focused on the authoritative basis for the property rights rather than on their specific characteristics.

Cross-referencing the two spectra allows for the identification of four types of property rights: private-individual, public-individual, public-group, and private-group. As explained in the following section, the last category is the best option (although the most rare and difficult to acquire legally) for protecting CBPRs, especially for original long-term occupants of a specific area.

Private Community-Based Property Rights

The ideal state-local community arrangement from the perspective of a typical local community would result in state recognition of private community-based property rights. Legal recognition of private CBPRs, however, would not imply exclusive authority. Private property rights are subject to state regulation and monitoring of the use of natural resources. The main benefit that local communities would gain from being legally recognized as private property rights holders would be more bargaining leverage with outside interests, including the government, than if their CBPRs were considered to be public property rights. The state, however, could still enact rural zoning laws over private CBPRs as it often does with regard to private individual property rights in urban areas.

Despite this state-zoning prerogative, private rights are typically stronger than public property rights and are more difficult to expropriate or allocate to other uses and/or users without due process and just compensation. While private property is subject to state regulation and can be seized by the state through eminent domain, this can only occur in order to serve the public interest and when due process requirements are followed. In Papua New Guinea, for example, where undocumented private CBPRs cover over 90% of the terrestrial land mass, local communities can legally oblige the government to consult with them and to win their cooperation before starting conservation or "development" initiatives. As private rights holders, they are also much better positioned to ensure that the government provides notice and due process, as well as just compensation, before their community-based rights are expropriated for public purposes.[16]

Western-oriented financial institutions, including the World Bank and the Asian Development Bank, determinedly promote individual privatization and direct so many resources to cadastral surveys and other means to disaggregate individual rights from CBPRs. They do this in the belief that lack of cognizable collateral restricts access to credit, which in turn restricts economic opportunity.[17]

The prevailing single-minded approach is based on a strong conviction that private individual property rights are preferable in most respects to public rights. This conviction, however, has not yet been extended to private group rights. This is because private group rights are not as easily marketed as private individual rights. An increasing amount of research, however, demonstrates that some natural resources are not best managed under individual property rights.[18] Yet there is still little acknowledgment that some natural resources such as watersheds, forests, and coastal areas are oftentimes better suited to and managed by common property and other forms of CBPRs.

The emphasis on individual titling is largely premised on a belief that it ensures security of tenure an thereby fosters entrepreneurial energy and in some cases even greed. Moreover, if everyone freely trades individual rights based on their own comparative advantage, everyone will end up better off than they were before trading. This system of trading is believed to promote the most productive, efficient use of land and, in turn, provides the greatest benefit to overall society (Ellsworth 2000).[19]

Usufruct agreements such as certificates, leases, or other restrictive tenurial instruments where the property rights remain public, are not so easily traded. They may nevertheless be appropriate in some circumstances, particularly with migrant groups whose rights and claims to natural resources are less strong and their local knowledge of natural resource management is less developed. In general, however, public tenure instruments are usually time-specific and often are not as conducive to the promotion of long-term sustainable objectives. They are vulnerable to arbitrary state cancellation, and as such they fail to provide leaseholders with adequate incentives to make the costly investments required to realize long-term gains.[20]

The simple fact is that private property rights—whether individual or community-based—are less easily canceled and less easily controlled by government. This is an important consideration in most majority world (developing) nations where state law is often hostile towards local communities directly dependent on natural resources. Private property rights also provide more leverage when negotiating with governments and outsiders such as commercial interests, and this is certainly a benefit that many poor rural communities could use.

Those who have a visceral, negative reaction to the concept of private, community-based rights should remember that *no property rights are absolute*, including private individual ones. No property rights are or presumably ever were completely free from some degree of governmental regulation in the public interest. Rather, all property rights within national boundaries, whether public or private, are subject to some degree of state regulation.

Furthermore, whether public or private, natural resource rights typically encompass a bundle of rights. Terms such as "ownership," "title," and "leasehold"—often used by outsiders to describe community-based tenurial rights—imply a Western concept of ownership that is often at odds with the principles and practices of community-based tenure and property rights. However, the element of ownership implicit in the concept of CBPRs should not be interpreted as an alien Western construct being imposed on local communities. Rather, it recognizes and respects the diversity and internally changing nature of indigenous resource management regimes. The concept is designed to help ensure that the local rights of natural resource users are respected. Often the only way to accomplish this successfully is to require that they be recognized as rightful owners.

It is important to emphasize that the concept of CBPRs is intended primarily for external application. It is meant to serve as a conceptual tool by clearly articulating an aspirational objective that is useful in negotiations with government and for communicating with external interests in clear and unequivocal terms.

Regardless of whether CBPRs are considered to be public or private, governments should work to help local communities promote sustainable management. Equitable zoning laws best exemplify this traditional governmental prerogative. Even in urban centers where private individual property rights (fee simple absolute) are commonplace, the state retains power to proscribe certain types of land use and development. Similar restraints could be established for the use of natural resources in rural areas, provided, of course, that they are in the public interest as broadly defined. Some legitimate concerns that would possibly merit zoning restrictions include seasonal migration, endangered species habitat, and watershed protection for downstream hydrology control.

CBPR Tenure Instruments and Legal Personalities

Recognizing CBPRs will, in most instances, require that local communities be defined in ways that are cognizable to national legal systems.[21] This will probably require in most instances that some type of documentary evidence be drafted. The task of defining local communities is best left to the communities themselves, although technical assistance is sometimes needed. Many local communities overlap. Some include conflicting factions and lack internal cohesion.[22] In order to resolve boundary conflicts with other communities, transparent dispute management processes need to be supported. Training in mediation should be provided to local governments and NGO actors.

In many, if not most cases, legal documents that provide evidence of CBPRs do not yet exist. As such, locally appropriate forms of evidence, for example, fallow fields, gravesites, orchards, and oral histories, should be accepted as evidence of indigenous ownership. Other admissible evidence could include census reports, tax receipts, and student rosters at local schools, as well as field research and other reports that substantiate assertions of original, long-term occupancy.

Locally appropriate evidence of indigenous ownership should create a legal presumption that the area is covered by CBPRs. This is fundamental. Without a legal presumption that areas known to be occupied by indigenous people and other long-term original inhabitants belong to them, state institutions responsible for issuing tenure instruments will be able to make unilateral and arbitrary determinations and prolong bureaucratic processes that are detrimental to local community interests.

As noted, local communities wishing to gain formal legal recognition of their CBPRs will need to acquire some form of recognized legal personality. This is typically done in the guise of cooperatives, village assemblies, or non-stock, non-profit corporations, all of which are contingent on state sanction and can be dissolved by the state. An alternative approach that would better protect the rights and interests of local communities would be for the legal personality of a community to be based on a census of all adult members, and not on legal documents that merely acknowledge the existence of a "people" or a formal state entity. In other words, any legal register of CBPRs should belong to the members of a community, and not to an ethnic group or formal state entity such as a corporation or cooperative.[23] If nothing else, a dual personality should be created so that if the state-sanctioned entity were dissolved, the CBPRs would not be deemed to have reverted back to the state. In any event, all local institutions involved in any CBNRM initiative should be transparent and accountable and should represent a significant percentage of any community being represented.

Promoting Enterprise Development

The issuance of any tenure instruments recognizing CBPRs should not be preconditioned on enterprise development and should also not preclude such development. Experience in the Philippines with forest cooperatives indicates that Indonesia would be wise to pursue an approach that accommodates local cultural and ecological variations. Whenever possible and as desired by communities themselves, peoples' organizations involved in community-based management projects should be based on pre-existing local institutions, including indigenous institutions and leadership systems. The most successful peoples' organizations, identified in a Philippine study funded by the U.S. Agency for International Development, were built on indigenous institutions representative of and respected by participating local communities (Lynch and Bonpin et al., forthcoming 2002).[24]

Legal and financial mechanisms for supporting enterprise development should also be separate from those used to recognize and secure CBPRs. Otherwise if a cooperative fails financially and is legally shut down, there is no "legal personality" left to hold the recognized CBPRs. As such, the CBPRs would necessarily revert back to the state, a problem discussed in the preceding section.

Summary

Community-based property rights encompass any rights that are derived from relationships, especially long-term ones, established between local peoples and the land and natural resources that sustain them. They draw their fundamental legitimacy from the community in which they operate, rather than from the nation-state in which they are located. Regardless of whether CBPRs cover private or public land and other natural resources, community members—not government officials or employees of NGOs, development institutions, or commercial enterprises—are the primary allocaters and enforcers of such rights.

The spread of free market economic policies in Indonesia and other developing countries is increasing pressures to exploit natural resources unsustainably and unjustly, particularly within areas covered by indigenous CBPRs. Increasing capital-intensive natural resource exploitation—including oil and mineral exploitation, bioprospecting activities, logging, agricultural expansion, and colonization by migrant settlers—is contributing to increasing environmental degradation, encroachment, and forced resettlement on indigenous peoples' territories. This report is premised on the conviction that these areas in Indonesia and the local communities that rely on them should be given priority attention if sustainable development and the national interest are to be effectively promoted. This includes rethinking and recognizing CBPRs and understanding how decentralization can be made more supportive of community-based management and ownership.

Notes

1. Marshall Alcorn, personal communication, August 2001. See, e.g., Derrida (1997, 1980) and Foucault (1972).

2. See, e.g., Rose (1994) for a discussion of political-economic discourse that supports a narrow interpretation of "property" as only transferable individual rights.

3. Although the reference may seem esoteric it merits emphasis that legal "rights" cannot exist unless there is also a corresponding "duty." However, common to widespread belief, this duty is not inherent in the rights holder. Rather, to possess a legal right someone or some institution (typically the government) has a duty to respect that right. In addition, there is no such thing as a legal right between a person and a thing. Rather, all legal rights are between persons. (See Hohfeld, 1913, 1917.) For example, people do not actually own land. Rather, they can own legal rights to land that other people and institutions have a duty to respect.

4. This does not, however, imply that such norms are uncontested or static.

5. In response to an earlier iteration of this position Daniel Bromley, a noted common property and economics scholar, argued that "While [legal] grant or recognition is both rare and bureaucratically cumbersome, effective resource management at the local level is impossible without it." See Box 4 at page 27 in Lynch and Talbott, *Balancing Acts*. In the opinion of the authors, this view is extreme and ignores a growing body of field research that conclusively demonstrates as much.

6. See Gollin and Kho (2001). The comment on page 23 states that, "Effective participation in the Philippines requires a focused effort to create and sustain conflict-management mechanisms that will help break the impasses, build consensus, and reach better decisions both within civil society itself and among civil society, the government, and the private sector. Interest-based negotiation and mediation are essential strategies in this effort. They provide a means of contributing to the empowerment of disadvantaged groups through negotiating on their own behalf. They also can enhance the effectiveness of civil society in participating in decision-making processes. This program approach is thus an important component of any strategy to support the growth of more equitable and participatory

systems for policy-making and the delivery of justice." On page 25 they add "Thus, it is crucial to develop a new process specifically geared towards coaching disadvantaged groups, so that they are able to effectively represent themselves in negotiations. This observation is equally true in Indonesia and the concept of CBPRs in intended to contribute to this new process. For more background on negotiation processes and rural communities see Li (1996), Scott (1990), and Edmunds and Nollenburg's document on power inequality in multi-stakeholder negotiations.

7. Ron Crocombe. "An Approach to the Analysis of Land Tenure Systems," in *Land Tenure in the Pacific*, Ron Crocombe, ed. (1971).

8. A related observation is that with commonly owned property, each owner makes his or her own decision about the use of the property according to his or her own needs. With collective property rights owned by a collective entity, such as a state or a corporation, formal decision-making processes are usually invoked. Property Law, 3 March 1998, University of Canberra. Available at: www.management.canberra.edu.au/lectures/law/sem981/unit3976/week1.html

9. The issue of how a local community might decide to sell or otherwise authorize external use of its natural resources is key. In Papua New Guinea, where private CBPRs are widely recognized, this issue has yet to be clearly resolved. In October 2001 the PNG judiciary did provide some guidance in a case involving CBPRs in Collingwood Bay.

10. See Reisman and Schreiber (1987), and Wignjosoebroto (1994).

11. Section 52 (d) of the Philippines Indigenous Peoples Rights Act (IPRA) of 1997 (Republic Act No. 8371) provides a listing of different types of evidence that can be used to prove the existence of indigenous CBPRs.

12. The Philippine Indigenous Peoples Rights Act (IPRA) provides for legal presumptions in favor of CBPRs within ancestral domains in sections 6, 55, and 57. Section 7 provides a listing of what these "rights of ownership and possession" entail.

13. For insights into the real tragedy of the commons, see Okoth-Ogendo 2000.

14. The content and nature of the bundle typically varies in all property rights. One typology identifies control (access), use, indirect economic gain, transfer, residual, and symbolic rights. See Crocombe (1971).

15. The concept of group rights at one end of the spectrum lacks precision because it is more expansive than just common property and can include individual rights. It does, however, facilitate the practical identification of the four prevailing types of property rights.

16. See Lynch and Marat (1992).

17. See de Soto (2001).

18. See the International Association for the Study of Common Property (IASCP) for more information: http://www.iascp.org, and Murphree (1996).

19. Ellsworth noted that promoters of "individual, private, tradable titles [believe they] are a precondition to economic growth and development. Moreover, property systems anchored in individual, tradable titles are in their view the best option around for managing all property. She added that the classic statement of this position is in Demsetz, 347–359 (1967). For the case of forests, a similar kind of argument is in Mendelsohn (1994). See also Bromley and Sjaastad (2000).

20. For an informative discussion of challenges posed by legally defining indigenous communities and other issues directly relevant to this report, see Colchester (2001).

21. Panayatou (1989). See also Bromley (1998).

22. For more information, see Li (1996).

23. The census of the local community can be updated periodically if necessary. Another option would be to rely on local *adat* institutions for ascertaining what rights children and other heirs inherit when listed community members die.

24. "Local Peoples and Public Interest Lawyers: Case Study Insights on Philippine National Law and Community-Based Natural Resources Management in the 1990s." Technical report submitted to the Philippine DENR and USAID Philippines, March 1999. Also available at: www.ciel.org.

II.

UNITY IN DIVERSITY?[1] COLONIAL AND POST-COLONIAL LEGAL LEGACIES

Throughout the world, nation-states have consolidated power by establishing territorial authority over land, subjects, and resources (Vandergeest and Peluso 1995; Mamdani 1996; Lynch and Talbott 1995; Lynch 1987; Thongchai 1994; Anderson 1987). In colonial states, the legal foundations of these strategies entailed various forms of Domain Declarations, assertions of vast claims of state ownership over land and other natural resources.[2] Claims of state jurisdiction over community resources in Indonesia began during the colonial era, continued under Sukarno, and were amplified under Suharto's centralized New Order Development State. As in many other nations, the state view of property ownership relied on a simple dichotomy of either individually owned private land or unowned land (*terra nullius*), the latter of which the state eventually claimed for itself. Traditional forms of community-based ownership, which at least implicitly legally recognized community-based group rights to land and other natural resources, ultimately had no place within the colonial system. By the end of the nineteenth century the Dutch colonial state, and then its national successors, claimed ownership over almost all land and resources covered by traditional CBPRs.

While there was some legal recognition of local diversity and *adat* (customary) law in Indonesia, concepts of local communities and community-based property rights were ignored in order to promote centralized state authority. Traditional *adat* principles, which generally hold that local community rights have priority over individual rights, were reinterpreted at the national level, so that national welfare trumped that of local communities and many individuals. National welfare and the common good were unilaterally defined by the state. These concepts were invoked to justify and promote rapacious economic development that arbitrarily expropriated CBPRs for the benefit of government and business elites. The resulting assertion of state legal jurisdiction over community land and other natural resources continues to the present day, a practice that ignores community-based property rights and criminalizes local customs and practices of resource use. This history of state policy and its increasing impact on traditional community institutions of resource management and governance is documented and analyzed in this chapter.

Village Governance under the Dutch State

The Dutch colonial presence in Indonesia initially began as a strictly commercial endeavor. Existing indigenous community rights and organization were tolerated and even recognized, *as long as* they did not conflict with colonial trade. Under the Netherlands East Indies Company (VOC), the Dutch colonial approach was as a company, not a state, and therefore took a mercantile approach to administration of the colonies. Emphasis was not on how to "govern" the colony but rather on how to efficiently extract its resources. The VOC intervened in local affairs only to assert and maintain control over lucrative resources and their trade. But the degree to which these resources were intertwined with local institutions meant that ultimately local law and practice was profoundly affected by colonial rule. As legal scholar Daniel Lev states:

> From the start, the VOC resolved to respect local law— another way of saying that, by and large, they could not have cared less—except where commercial interests were at stake. What they did not respect, and given their ambitions could not, were local economic and political relationships— always fundamental sources of local law (Lev 1985: 58).

When the VOC charter expired in 1800, the Dutch state took over colonial governance. Since the VOC made few attempts outside of the teak-rich areas of Java and Madura to control native administration directly or to claim sovereignty over native territory, much of the colony remained under indigenous self-rule. In the interest of establishing a courts system under the new state administration, Governor-General Deandels (1808–1811) formed the first Dutch-recognized native court.[3] Each prefecture was presided over by native elites who were known as Regents in the service of the Dutch (Hooker 1975). Although deeply flawed by colonial manipulation of local leadership and decision-making, the theory behind the native courts was to practice legal pluralism and to respect the differences in local customary law (Hooker 1975 251–253). Ultimately, however well-intentioned, this intervention helped to facilitate colonial rule through the control of local institutions.

Additionally, the Constitutional Regulations (*Regerings Reglement*) of 1836 and 1854 recognized and ostensibly aimed to safeguard customary rights to virgin land and forest products as well as pre-existing community institutions and governance (Hooker 1975; Zerner 1990; Safitri 1999).[4] As provided in Article 71,

> [T]he Village, except as agreed upon by authorities indicated by national regulations, has a village headman (*kepala desa*) and a village government (*pemerintah desa*). The Governor-General protects this right. The *kepala desa* makes regulations regarding the management of households in accordance with national and regional regulations and the unity of the community.

These regulations only applied to Java and Madura, where the *desa* was understood to be an indigenous organization and not (initially) a term for the most local form of state administration. They were not an attempt to create a uniform local governmental entity throughout the archipelago; that would occur later.

Colonial Usurpations and Local Responses

The comprehensive legal assault on community-based property rights and institutions in Indonesia commenced during the Napoleonic Wars, which included a brief period of rule known as the British Interregnum (1811–1816). At that time, the British Governor-General, Sir Thomas Raffles instituted a land rent[5] system that was to be calculated according to household land holdings. To calculate land rent, it was necessary to investigate native tenure, which Raffles misunderstood to have nothing in common with private ownership. In a harbinger of widespread future thinking, Raffles equated private ownership with western notions of individual title and overlooked diverse native concepts of community-based property rights and control. Raffles decided that in the absence of private individual ownership, the native populations held only usufruct rights. In 1813, he issued a proclamation that declared, "Proprietary rights to land in Java were vested in the sovereign and in the European Government as the successor of the Javanese sovereigns." (Ball 1982; Hooker 1978).

To ensure an expansive interpretation of the Raffles Declaration, any land not currently under tillage or that had lain fallow for more than three years was considered unowned "wasteland" (Peluso 1992, 64). This became a classic British colonial tactic that was also applied in Ceylon, India, and elsewhere (Lynch and Talbott 1995). Raffles also decided that the village (*desa*) was the basic unit of administration throughout the entire archipelago, and therefore the headman, who was perceived to represent the village, could be made an agent of the administration (Hooker 1975; Bremen 1982). This misperception and the conceptual homogenization of diverse local communities and their forms of leadership marked the beginning of an ongoing and nearly two-centuries-long manipulation of local institutions and authority throughout the vast archipelago.

When the Dutch returned to the Netherlands East Indies (NEI) in 1816, the new Governor-General issued a proclamation that declared that British laws on land rights were to remain in force. The Dutch, however, amended Raffles' earlier decree so that community-based land rights would be recognized, provided they did not interfere with European sovereignty (Ball 1982).

Misapprehensions of native systems of rights and governance, meanwhile, inspired Professor Van Vollenhoven (1906–1933) to establish a Centre of *Adat* Studies in Leiden. Van Vollenhoven sought to document community-based legal systems as a strategy for promoting legal recognition of village governance under local systems of *adat*. One of the principle aims of Van Vollenhoven's *adat* documentation was to create legally cognizable evidence of the variety of local legal institutions.[6] This included an intent to undermine Raffles' assertion that fallow land was not covered by community rights and therefore belonged to the colonial sovereign. His research demonstrated that under most local tenure systems outside of Java, land rights held by local people who moved away or died without heirs were not considered to have been abandoned. Rather, these rights reverted to the local community and were understood to remain in a commonly held pool (Holleman 1981).

Domain Declarations and the Agrarian Law of 1870

Eventually, Raffles' assertion of colonial ownership and control over natural resources was subsequently expanded and systematically routinized throughout the Indonesian islands. The Dutch Cultivation System was established in 1830 and required local residents in direct rule areas to pay exorbitant land "rents" (again implying their lack of ownership) in the form of export crops. Many local people were forced to neglect or abandon subsistence crops in order to produce enough to meet arbitrarily imposed quotas. Consequently, during the 1840s, famines wracked many local communities in Java, and popular resistance mounted along with nationalist sentiment. In response to these famines and rising popular agitation, the state prohibited the sale of land rights to non-Indonesians through the Agrarian Law of 1870.[7] The putative rationale behind the law was to provide food security, assuring that a sufficient amount of arable land remained under native Indonesian control.

More important for the colonists, the Agrarian Law was meant to promote the expansion of private investment in natural resource industries, especially in plantation agriculture. As such, the Agrarian Law allowed private investors in export crop production to lease lands from the colonial state. Community-based property rights were only recognized on continuously cultivated land, while other land was declared to be "waste land" (Peluso 1992). Reinforcing Raffles' declaration, the Agrarian Law declared that all "unclaimed" or "waste land" in the direct rule areas of Java and Madura was the property of the state, a proclamation known as the *Domeinverklaring,* or Domain Declaration.[8] This contributed in a significant way to the consequent erosion of local sovereignty, which the State conceptually simplified and made uniform. Traditional rights and institutions were ultimately ignored, an approach that has largely continued uninterrupted through the post-New Order era.

The domain declarations were tempered by some recognition of native rights to land. "Unfree" (under continuous cultivation) land, was differentiated from "waste land" and deemed unavailable to the colonial state. Further, the Dutch Constitution of 1848 specified two roles for the regime: to collect land revenue, and to preserve native welfare (Peluso and Vandergeest n.d., 20). The competing purposes of revenue and preservation of native welfare illustrate the tension in the Dutch vision of legitimate state control. "[T]hus at this early date, native welfare was already part of the colonial state's ideology— however badly they accomplished it" (Ibid).

The practice of declaring land not under continuous cultivation as "unowned" and as the property of the state had its most dramatic impacts in the Outer Islands. Whereas in much of Java, permanent wet-rice cultivation on rich volcanic soils was the norm, throughout the Outer Islands, low population densities and poor soils made long-fallow swidden agriculture the common practice. Because most land in the Outer Islands was not continually cultivated, vast tracts could be claimed by the colonial state as "wasteland." Use of domain declarations to establish direct rule in more areas of the Outer Islands was attempted in the later 1870s and 1880s, but this was met with great controversy within the Dutch government itself.

Uncertainty ensued over the nature of community-based tenure in the Outer Islands, the suitability of swidden cultivation versus "continuous cultivation," and who were the most appropriate managers of forest resources (Potter 1988). In 1924, the first state forest reserves (established primarily on hydrological criteria) were classified in the Outer Islands. The actual demarcation of "reserved" or "unclassified" forests was slow to proceed because of internal debates within the state as well as technological, topographical, and personnel difficulties. Some information was recorded, much of it inaccurate or incomplete (Peluso and Vandergeest n.d.). Later, however, this information provided rhetorical justification for assertions of state sovereignty over forest reserves that had been "mapped" (Li 1999). This, in turn, heralded the beginning of "forest" demarcation,[9] according to the state's view of ecological, economic and social functions,[10] a particular view of forests that would persist into and beyond the independent New Order.

Debates about the applicability of agrarian laws in the Outer Islands raged on within the Dutch Government until the onset of World War II, after which state attention focused on resisting the movement for independence. These debates contribute to vagueness in the laws that were promulgated (DepHut 1986), and the ambiguity was later used to foster an expansive interpretation in favor of state ownership and authority. Ironically, state claims were most expansive after independence.

Redefining Territory and Resource Rights

Under Dutch rule, natural resources such as animal and forest products were controlled either through trade regulations (by establishing a state monopoly or a system of fees and licenses) or by reducing legal access to spatial areas in which the resources were found, that is, within concessions issued by the state. Efforts to control the use of natural resources either by regulating the trade of valuable species or by regulating the activities in a geographic area resulted in widespread erosion of community-based rights to natural resources (Vandergeest and Peluso 1995, n.d.). Regulating activities in a geographic area was a means of simplifying diverse community-based rights to various natural resources by defining them within a specific area.

The stringency of colonial regulation of natural resources (and thereby interference with CBPRs) was largely determined by the relative value of the trade (Potter 1988; Dove 1993a, 1996). The products of most interest to the Dutch VOC were teak and spices (clove, nutmeg, cinnamon, and pepper). The exclusive spaces created for the extraction of these products was subsequently expanded to create plantations, not only of teak and spices, but also of rubber, tea, sugar, coffee, tea, tobacco, gambier, and quinine. Other resource rights converted to territorial (i.e., land) rights included *ramin* and ironwood in Kalimantan, *jelutung* (native latex) concessions in East and South Kalimantan (Potter 1988), and tin, gold, coal, silver, and oil in Kalimantan and Sumatra (Lindblad 1988).

In addition, game reserves for wildlife and nature reserves were also established (Staatsblad 1905). Initially these reserves prohibited hunting of tropical birds, but later their coverage was expanded to cover all mammals and birds in the wild, except for research (Cribb

1988, 1997; Peluso and Vandergeest n.d.). The Game Ordinance of 1931 further bureaucratized game hunting by establishing hunting seasons, licenses, and allowable techniques and weapons for hunting (Peluso and Vandergeest n.d.). Through these enactments, legal access to natural resources became increasingly restricted and ever more regulated by national law rather than local community-based law.

Redefining the Village and Increasing State Intervention Following Independence

The independence movement that ended Dutch colonial rule declared success in 1945 (although it would take several more years of protracted fighting until the Dutch conceded). The end of colonial rule was immediately followed by efforts of the new Indonesian government to foster national unity and later to facilitate economic growth. From independence to the present, however, traditional village political organizations and CBPRs to natural resources have been legally circumscribed and undermined by state-centric strategies that also contribute to the erosion of local institutions and leadership.

This is a striking development in light of Article 18 of the Indonesian constitution, especially before its amendment in 2000. It specifically recognized the presence and status of local governance institutions. The official explanation of the article stated:

> [T]here are roughly 250 types of self governing villages (*Zelfbesturende landschappen*) and native communities (*volksgemeenschappen*) such as *desa* on Java and Bali, *negeri* in Minangkabau and *dusun* and *marga* in Palembang and so on. These areas have their own indigenous organizational structures (*susunan asli*) and because of them can be construed as areas with special attributes (*daerah yang bersifat istimewah*). The State of the Republic of Indonesia respects the status of these special areas and all the state regulations concerning them shall heed the original hereditary rights (*hak-hak asal-usul*) of these areas. (Indonesian Constitution of 1945, Official Explanation, Chapter IV, Article 18, Section 2.)

Despite this constitutional recognition of the diversity and rights of native communities, national policy has continuously emphasized village uniformity and control by the centralized government. This was in part because the new nation of Indonesia was geographically vast and culturally varied, and early nationalists thought that strong central control and a focus on unity were crucial for national coherence.

During the final months of his presidency, President Sukarno passed the Law on Village Governance and Jurisdiction (UU 19/1965 *Desapradja*). This law replaced colonial laws acknowledging the status of indigenous social units, with a mandate requiring villages to be administratively uniform. In clear contradiction to the constitutional principle of respecting local villages' institutional diversity, the law mandated national uniformity by engineering the composition, size, and administrative institutions of all villages, thereby overriding community-based forms of social organization. Like other village administrative laws that followed, this law emphasized the village as an administrative body of the central government and downplayed the importance of traditional villages as social or territorial units.

Soon after taking power in 1965, the new President Suharto declared Sukarno's village governance law (UU 19/1965, described above) as unconstitutional. However, in 1979, he then decreed his own unconstitutional version of village uniformity, in the form of the Law on Village Government (UU 5/1979). The administrative village, or *desa,* became the basic unit of development under Suharto's New Order. Only recently repealed under decentralization in 1999, this law was the most crippling assault ever on village authority in Indonesia. In place for twenty years, its effects continue to endure.

The national concept of *desa* was a foreign idea outside of Java and Madura. Nevertheless, the New Order state designated *desa* boundaries based on the Dutch understanding of Javanese villages[11] and placed these new administrative units directly below the *kecamatan* (sub-district). This "clarification" further confused matters already muddled during the colonial era. Outside of Java, communities were typically more territorially expansive than (and not politically subordinate to) the *kecamatan*. Nor were they necessarily politically subordinate to the *kabupaten* (district), province, or even the nation-state. Provincial development funds, however, were allocated to administrative districts based on their total number of *desa*. To better access development funds from the central government, provincial governors opted to enforce the uniform definition of *desa* held by the state—that is, a demographic and administrative unit, rather than a community-based one with any functional legal autonomy.

The legal definition of the "village" in the 1979 Law on Village Administration added three more important implications (Safitri 1999). First, it required that residents be considered in a strictly demographic way—as a grouping of people based on population size and quantifiable characteristics, not on any customary pattern of social cohesion, functional governance, or territorial control. Second, the law converted villages into an administrative (not political or cultural) unit, subordinate to the *Camat* and part of the national bureaucracy. Lastly, it did not provide traditional village communities with any right to control their own affairs. This last provision severed community-based village autonomy and firmly established the central state's authority over village lives and natural resources.

Despite this attempt to impose a centralized and externally imposed form of village leadership, community-based rights and village institutions in many places throughout Indonesia endured. Many still manifest an array of specialized institutions and positions, including leaders in spiritual and health matters, agricultural and resource management, and dispute mediation and adjudication. While a political hierarchy can still be found within some traditional institutions, in many locales, leadership positions continue to be traditionally mediated by public participation, support and open debate. In such cases, this helps to ensure that local leadership is more responsive to community goals and needs. Rather than asserting a monopoly of authority, local leadership is often diffuse and relies on consultation and challenge by different community authorities (as documented in case studies[12] by Palijama, Maelissa, Kanyan, Jaelani, Giay, Supit, and Puru Bebe).

Uniformity of centralized authority and local institutions introduced under the new *kepala desa* was a dramatic and externally imposed change in leadership for many local communities. Villages were— and still are—defined by abstract statistics that can be tallied and managed (case studies by Maelissa; Giay; Supit; Dalip and Priyana; Kanyan; Laudjeng and Ramlah; see also Scott 1998; Zakaria 2000). This uniform concept of "village" under the New Order was designed to impose state control.[13] As President Sukarnoputri observed in 1997, while she was outside the government and campaigning for *reformasi,* "We have directed our attention entirely to Unity, and failed to do anything substantial to give meaningful expression to Diversity within our daily life as a nation." (Sukarnoputri 1997).

Diverse indigenous concepts of community (such as the longhouse of some Kalimantan *Dayak* groups, Mentawai *uma*, Pakava *ngata*, Balinese *banjar* or *seray* in some Paupuan indigenous groups, etc.) are not defined by spatial location (or geographic coordinates) or demography (the number of residents, households, etc.), as is uniformly required under state administration. Rather, indigenous concepts of village communities include territorial authorities and social units with ties (usually of family) between people, who often move about according to farming cycles, fishing and hunting seasons, or wage labor journeys. By considering villages as merely an administrative unit defined by an aggregation of demographic data, the local importance of these traditional social and cultural ties is undermined. Furthermore, the natural resources within village territories are conveniently considered to be beyond any purview of CBPRs, making them—as far as the state is concerned—public goods that are not legally encumbered.

The 1979 Law on Village Administration also dramatically circumscribed the powers of local officials in charge of state defined villages. It authorized only a few individuals to act and speak for entire communities, an unprecedented development in many locales. It also defined who could hold those positions of power. The *kepala desa,* or village headmen,[14] were vetted (if not virtually appointed) by the *Camat* or *Bupati* (sub-district and district heads) who could likewise remove them from office. The appointment of village headman was contingent on "special research" (*penelitian khusus*) that determined their suitability. Suitability was determined by political affiliations (including a disqualification of those with possible "communist" associations) and familiarity with *Pancasila* ideology.[15] As a direct result, village leaders were more accountable to the officials who appointed them than to the local communities they purportedly represented.

The 1979 law on village administration ignored existing community-based forms and processes of village decision-making, many of which provided for open debate and participation (case studies by Palijama; Maelissa; Kanyan; Jaelani). It created an official legislative body (*Lembaga Musyawarah Desa,* or LMD), and provided that

29

decisions by the LMD were subject to approval by the *Bupati*. The LMD was based on an introduced idea of executive and legislative balance of power, yet this balance was negated by regulations allowing village headmen to chair the body and the other (government-appointed) administrative officers to also sit on the board. The pseudo-democratic nature of the institution was further corrupted by the requirement that all village officers and members of the LMD be members of the ruling party, GOLKAR.[16] The latter requirement served to preclude any alternative village-level political organizations. As a result, rather than providing for democratic representation, the law narrowed power and overrode existing checks and balances.

This much authority was channeled to the *kepala desa* because the *desa* had become the fundamental bureaucratic unit, and compliant headmen were needed to "implement" (through coercion if necessary) central government's policies and programs. State plans included national development through the establishment of capital-intensive natural resource extraction industries.

Tightly regulated village leadership subordinate to centralized government control could also emasculate independent community autonomy and vitality. In fact, this is precisely what the 1979 Village Law sought to accomplish (case studies by Maelissa; Supit; Kanyan; see also Zakaria 2000). Traditional community-based village institutions were further undermined and even criminalized under the Ministry of Interior Regulation on Villages No.4/1981. It proscribed the inclusion of any *desa* within a state forest area or HGU (*hak guna usaha*, which means concession). Traditional communities located inside "state-owned" forests areas were legally banned, and many residents were involuntarily relocated, their CBPRs arbitrarily ignored and overridden. As recently as the mid to late 1990s, relocations were accompanied by violence and military operations. Involuntary displacements in South Sumatra forced thousands of people from their homes, and their houses and crops were burned[17] or trampled by trained elephants (Fay et al. 1999; see also Bachriadi n.d.). Throughout Indonesia, CBPRs to natural resources, even indigenous ones, were ignored and those who held and asserted them were subject to criminal arrest (see Fay et al. 1999; Peluso 1992; Peluso and Vandergeest n.d).[18]

In another effort to sever community-based rights and to assert state claims over land and other natural resources, the Ministry of

Social Affairs directed a program that commenced in the 1950s to resettle an estimated 160,000 people considered to be "primitive."[19] This was purportedly done to provide access to "modern" villages and government services and to remove a danger to the natural environment.[20] This type of resettlement, however, was frequently followed by the appropriation of village land rights for transmigration, logging, plantations, or mining (case studies by Laudjeng, Jaleani; see also Colchester 1986).

The case studies and other research relied on in this report also provide evidence that the erosion of community-based institutions and their ties to local leaders fostered collusion between many appointed village headmen and commercial concessionaires. With community-based institutions under assault, a crisis of confidence in state appointed village headmen further weakened the cohesion of many local communities and their traditional practices of natural resource management.

Independence, *Adat,* and the Constitution

Adat, or local custom and law, is not static. Nor does it pass unchanged from generation. *Adat* is complex and dynamic. It has a deeply politicized history of interpretation, which can only briefly be touched on in this report.[21] As Indonesian independence and nationalism dawned, *adat* took on special significance as the "original law," "the people's law." *Adat* was understood to provide an appropriate foundation for the new Indonesian nation, as it was derived from everyday experience and norms, not from decrees imposed by the colonial state. The diversity of *adat* cultures was understood by nationalist leaders to be an integral part of what made the new nation of Indonesia unique and legitimate. Support for this diversity was believed to strengthen national unity.

During the constitutional debates of the 1940s and 1950s, the *adat* law scholar Soepomo argued that sovereignty should be in the hands of the Indonesian people (see Article 1, Section 2 of the Constitution). Soepomo believed in the unity of individuals and society under *adat* (Nasution 1992). He searched for what was unique and fundamental about Indonesia and concluded that *adat* should be the basis of the new Constitution and the new legal system (Koesnoe 1992; Soepomo 1951; Yamin 1959).[22] Developing a concept of national cultural heritage and history, he argued that the new nation-state should be based on a unified idea of the "*adat* principles" of consensus and common good rather than "western" ideas of majority rule and individual rights. Ultimately Soepomo's ideas on the uniformity of *adat* prevailed and the Second Constitutional Council (MPRS) decreed *adat* as the "original law" which· provided the constitutional foundation of the Republic of Indonesia.

The interpretation of *adat* principles to promote national unity pursuant to a concept of uniformity rather than diversity was ironic (Koesnoe 1976). It led to a belief that under "national *adat*" community rights have priority over individual rights and that only one community mattered, the Republic of Indonesia. However well intentioned during the 1940s and 1950s, this novel and politically motivated interpretation would be invoked to explain away ensuing widespread injustice and disaffection.

National *adat* was central to the idea of a "*Pancasila* Democracy" in which the "common good" would be ultimately determined by the "father" (read: President) of the "family" (read: Nation) rather than by majority vote (read: Western).[23] The New Order "Integralist" idea saw the state and the nation as being inseparable, a vision that was to contribute to interpretations of Constitutional principles that upheld state authority while undermining local community-based authorities (Sopoemo, cited in Yamin 1959, 114–119). It highlighted the transformation of *adat* as the icon of diversity into *adat* as a unifying and uniform National Heritage of the entire Indonesian citizenry (Lev 1985; Burns 1989).

Legal Recognition of *Adat* CBPRs under Existing Law

The first law enacted following independence (after the protracted constitutional debates concluded) was the Basic Agrarian Law (BAL) No. 5/1960.[24] This law, which is proof of the importance of land rights in Indonesian history, was explicitly intended to erase remnants of colonial agrarian laws, to foster national unity, and to lay the foundations for land reforms that would benefit the rural populace (Official Explanation, Chapter 1 of the General Elucidation). Unfortunately, as interpreted by Suharto's New Order state the law produced little real change.[25]

Nevertheless, the BAL provides support for the legal recognition of *adat* CBPRs (*hak ulayat*).[26] It explicitly allows for the registration of *adat* territories[27] and recognizes *adat* law, rather than colonial Western law, as the primary basis for land ownership. Article 5 declares that "*adat* law applies to land, water and air, as long as those rights do not conflict with national interest...." The Official Explanation (Chapter 3, Section 1) states that under Article 5 "Novel agrarian law must be appropriate to the people's law. Because most people live by *adat* law, the new agrarian law must be based on *adat* law as the original law...."

The mandate for recognition of *adat* CBPRs in the BAL is admittedly muddied by the qualification that they must not contradict the interests of the state and the nation of the new Indonesia as a whole. The law opens in Article 1 with the declaratory statement that

> [A]ll land, water and natural resources, including underground resources with the Republic of Indonesia have been granted by God and *are the land, water and natural resources of the Indonesian people and have become a national asset.* (Article 1, Section 1-2; emphasis added).

The official explanation for this provision emphasizes the paramount importance of "the common good" over community-based property rights. It states that

> [T]he land, water and air within the sovereign territory of independent Indonesia was fought for by all citizens, and therefore has become the common property of the entire nation, not solely of private owners or indigenous inhabitants. This interpretation grants a customary common property right (*hak ulayat*) of the highest order held by the Indonesian nation. (Official Explanation, General Provisions, Section 2, Part 1).

This interpretation subordinates *adat* CBPRs and implies that Indonesia is also "open access" to all of its citizens. Equally important, it provides no support for the narrow interpretation of "national interest" as synonymous with commercial enterprise, as was the case during the New Order regime. Unfortunately, while ostensibly intended to promote national well being, the still prevailing, New Order interpretation of the BAL undermined national diversity by promoting a uniform, state-centric definition of the "national interest" that benefited commercial enterprises at the expense of local communities. (For an alternative definition of the national interest, see Chapter VI.)

Implementing regulations for the BAL were never promulgated, political instability and the overthrow of Sukarno's administration being two key factors.[28] As a result, few people were ever aware that their *adat* CBPRs could be registered. Meanwhile, because the BAL also reaffirmed the state's constitutional right to all "unowned" land and other natural resources, the official interpretation contributed to further expropriation of local rights, an outcome that was *opposite* the law's original intent (case studies by Supit; Laudeng and Ramlah).

The BAL's vague limitation on *adat* rights was essentially invoked by the New Order to assert that *adat* rights contradict the "national interest." Under Suharto's Integralist state, the "common good" became synonymous with economic development, which directly benefited the government and business elite rather than "the nation" (Barber 1986; Peluso 1992; Peluso and Vandergeest n.d.). Although explicitly based on recognition of the primacy of *adat* law and ownership and a desire to end any legal dualism between Western and *adat* law, the BAL has so far failed to contribute to the development of any consensus on the nature of *adat* rights. Rather, the official interpretation of the law still contributes to dependence on an imported Western paradigm of development that harms local communities.

The possibility of a democratic and environmentally just interpretation of the BAL nevertheless endures. As of 2001, the BAL still allows for the legal recognition of *adat* CBPRs.

Besides the BAL, other major natural resource laws in Indonesia specifically recognize *adat* CBPRs and local communities' right to participate in resource planning. The Basic Planning Law,[29] the Basic Forestry Law, and various environmental laws all acknowledge local rights to land and other natural resources, as well as the right of citizens to participate in management. For example, as with its predecessor (UUPK 5/1967), the new Basic Forestry Law (UUPK 41/1999, Article I, Section 6) recognizes the existence of *adat* rights within state forests. Further, it mandates respect for customary laws provided they do not contradict national interests (Article 4 (3)).

Other national environmental laws specifically acknowledge that all citizens have the right to a clean and safe environment and the right to participate in environmental management.[30] Despite these legal guarantees of participation, local communities are rarely consulted, a sad fact documented by many of the case studies discussed in Chapter III.

New Order Resource Management and the New Domain Declarations

Government efforts to manage natural resources in Indonesia are largely sectoral. Different laws are regulated and implemented by different Ministries. The Ministries of Forestry and Estate Crops (and sub-directorate of Conservation), Agriculture (and sub-directorate of Fisheries), Energy and Mining, and Environment often compete for jurisdiction. The newly established Ministry of Marine Affairs has just begun to join in the competition. Yet, all of these institutions show similarities in their legal approaches, and in many ways highlight the tension between state control and local rights present in the Constitution.

The prevailing interpretation of Indonesia's basic natural resource laws invokes the legacy of the colonial Domain Declarations. It gives the central state an exclusive legal right to control most natural resources, including attendant rights to authorize access and use. Pursuant to this assertion of overarching state authority, large-scale commercial extraction is prioritized, while local subsistence and small-scale commercial farmers, fishers, and miners who practice their livelihoods in traditional areas are deemed criminals.[31] Furthermore, while national laws mandate that natural resources be used for the benefit of all citizens (as based on the 1945 Constitution, as revised), these laws and their implementation have not led to the sustainable use of natural resources or to he improved welfare of millions of Indonesian citizens.

Under the prevailing interpretation, the constitutional basis for the expansive state assertion of natural resource ownership is Article 33. Section 3 provides that

> [T]he land, the waters and the natural richness contained therein shall be controlled by the State and exploited to the greatest benefit of the people.

Forest Resources (Including Estate Crops and Protected Areas)

Article 33 is reiterated in the language of the Basic Forestry Laws of 1967 and 1999. The 1967 law stated that "all forests within the territory of the Republic of Indonesia, and all the resources they contain, are under the authority of the state" (Article 5, Basic Forestry Law No 5/ 1967). The 1999 reiteration provides that "all forests within the territory of the Republic of Indonesia including all the richness contained therein are under the state's control for people's maximum welfare," (Article 4 (1)).

These forestry laws promote sweeping reconfigurations of state authority and ownership, as well as *adat* law, CBPRs, and even the concept of forest. These reconfigurations do more than contradict *adat* law. They bolster an unconstitutional expansion of state power and the erosion of local rights and welfare, as well as the welfare of forests—all of which are explicitly protected under the Constitution.

Like the forest classifications of the colonial past, under both basic forest laws, all land in Indonesia is divided into privately owned forest (*hutan milik*) and state forest (*hutan negara*), which is therefore implied to be "unowned." The official explanation for this in the 1967 law asserts that "state forests are all those which are not private property (*tidak dibebani hak milik*), including those under customary law," thereby denying that customary law is a form of private ownership. (Article 2, Official Explanation, General Elucidation; emphasis added.)

Nevertheless, the 1967 law also explicitly recognized the existence of *adat* law and rights within those categories:

> The inclusion of forests under the control of indigenous communities within state forest *does not annul the respective rights of the indigenous community to make, use or obtain benefits from the forest*, to the extent that those rights still exist. (Article 2, Official Explanation, General Elucidation; emphasis added.)

Further, Article 17 recognized the existence of *adat* CBPRs to "among others, forest exploitation, cattle tending, wild game hunting, and forest products collection,"[32] as long as they are not in contradiction with the protection and production of forests.[33] As an affirmation of local capacities to use forests without compromising these goals, Article 15 further recognized local communities as assets in forest management and protection and mandated their responsibility to participate in these activities.

Despite the mandate of local participation, prevailing interpretations of Articles 13 and 14 in the 1967 forestry law supported assertions of exclusive state authority over the regulation and control of State Forests, including the right to grant this authority to private or state commercial entities. The law thereby implicitly gave priority to production forestry (Official Explanations of Article 17, Article 6, and Article 5) and prioritized the interests of industry over all others (case studies by Kanyan; Laudjeng and Ralmah; Puru Bebe; Mealissa). For example, the official interpretation of the law states that "all activities exploiting the natural richness of Indonesia which materialize in the forms of forest, are aimed to develop the national economy in the shortest period possible...."[34] This interpretation further expands the state's authority to allocate and define the meaning, function, and uses of land and forest resources, as well as defining the "national interest." These interpretations in favor of the prioritization of commercial interests and broad state authority have worked to diminish community rights—including rights to ancestral domains and the equal rights of Indonesian citizens to access and participation in natural resource management. They have served as the legal engine of Indonesian forest policy since the beginning of the New Order and continue to operate largely undisturbed today.

In addition to the use of economic development as a synonym for national interest, the second tier of the New Order state's tactics was to assert that local *adat* systems were no longer functional. The New Order state established a monopoly on determining the existence of community rights and the functionality of customary law systems, a monopoly that likewise endures in the Post–New Order era. For example, a 1998 Ministerial Decree[35] states that the existence of *adat* rights and legal systems are to be determined solely by a governor's proclamation.

The use of arbitrary government criteria for determining whether customary rights are still in effect allows pre-existing CBPRs to be ignored. For example, the forest laws empower the ministry to determine the "uses and function" of forest resources through the designation of large areas as "Protected," "Production," or "Conversion" forests, regardless of their use or ownership by local communities (case studies by Kanyan; Puru Bebe; Jaelani; Lumintang; Giay). The nontransparent and unaccountable process by which community rights are addresses fosters abuse and corruption, as demonstrated by the case studies and numerous writings on Indonesian military involvement in the forest sector (Peluso 1993; Barr 1998; Lowry 1996; Barber and Talbott 2001).

Unfortunately, little was changed in regards to the legal recognition of *adat* CBPRs in the new Revised Forest Law of 1999, except for Article 5. It provides in paragraph 2 that "*adat* forest shall be determined as long as it exists in reality and its existence is recognized." This new proviso seems to allow for a new category of state forestland that will be classified as *adat* forest. As of January 2002, however, no implementing regulation has been promulgated. In addition, proponents of *adat* rights vehemently object to the notion that *adat* CBPRs are subordinated to state ownership or subject to state criteria. These advocates call for the legal recognition of *adat* rights as being community owned.

Mining and Mineral Resources

The Basic Mining Law, No. 11/1967, followed the same colonial principles as the Basic Forestry Law, but to an even greater degree. In Article 1, the mining law reiterates the Domain Declarations by stating that "all deposits ... are national assets to be controlled and used by the state for the common good." Further, the law prioritizes large mining operations, because small community mining is not considered capable of contributing to economic growth (Article 8). Only small deposits are made accessible for community operations (Article 11). Of course, if nothing valuable is made available for community management, no large contribution can possibly be made (case study by Sukanto)! Finally, Article 26 requires concessionaires to notify local rights holders (which the case studies demonstrate is not usually done). Even when adhered to, this notification is little more than a formality. The mining law is the most strident of all the resource laws in prioritizing commercial extraction in that it *specifically requires* that local people relinquish their CBPRs to commerical mining operations. This requirement, however, conflicts with democratic principles and the recognized primacy of *adat* rights in the Indonesian Constitution (case studies by Palijama; Sukanto; Sitianpessy; Supit).

Fisheries and Coastal and Marine Resources

The competition between different Ministries is also evident in coastal and marine resource management. This sector is plagued by existing

---

Box 1. Yosepha Alomang and Freeport McMoRan

"Freeport is digging out our mother's brain. That is why we are resisting."
—An indigenous Amungme resident

"We have a volcano that's been decapitated by nature, and we're mining the esophagus, if you will."
"We are thrusting the spear of development into the heart of Irian Jaya."
—Freeport McMoRan CEO Jim Bob Moffet

The violence of this imagery epitomizes the physical and environmental violence that Freeport McMoRan has brought to the West Papuan people. For over 20 years Yosepha Alomang, a member of the indigenous Amungme tribe of West Papua, has been fighting the world's largest gold and copper mine owned by U.S.-based Freeport McMoRan and located on a mountain the Amungme believe is sacred. Freeport's 30 years of mining in West Papua on Amungme land have caused forced displacement, destruction of rainforests and rivers, and countless human rights violations.

Freeport contends that, "the land within Freeport's 'Contract of Work Area,' like almost all land in Indonesia, is legally *tanah negara* (state-owned land) under the terms of the Indonesian Constitution." Under the 'Contract of Work' with the government, Freeport has been granted clear legal right to use specified areas to conduct our operations during the term of the contract." Meanwhile, the Amungme have watched the

(Box continued on next page)

Box 1 (continued)

sacred mountain disappear because of strip mining. The Ajkwa Riverplants that grow near it. Each day over 200,000 tons of tailings are is so polluted from the mine that Kwamki-lama residents have been warned by Freeport's own employees to not drink the water or eat deposited in the river. The U.S. Federal government cancelled political risk insurance it provided Freeport in 1995 because of the tailings, stating that the mine "created and continues to pose unreasonable or major environmental, health or safety hazards with respect to the rivers that are being impacted by the tailings, surrounding terrestrial ecosystem and the local inhabitants."

However, Freeport is the largest source of tax revenue in Indonesia and has therefore long benefited from the support of the government and military forces.

Peaceful protests against the company have been brutally suppressed by the military. In 1994 "Mama Yosepha" was arrested for allegedly giving support to West Papuans resisting Freeport and Indonesian military forces. She was tortured and interrogated for six weeks, including being held for one week without food or drink in a room knee-deep with water and human waste. Despite these abuses, she has continued to be an outspoken community leader, raising awareness of the cultural and environmental destruction, human rights abuses, and government and military collusion associated with Freeport's operations. For her courageous efforts and tireless activism, she was awarded the prestigious Goldman Environmental Prize in 2001.

Despite the enormous power that Freeport wields, recent court rulings against the mining company have shown positive signs for environmental justice. In August 2001, the South Jakarta District Court ruled against PT Freeport Indonesia for environmental damage and covering up the deaths of four mine workers in a May 2000 accident involving the collapse of a tailings dump. The judge ordered Freeport to follow Bappedal (Environmental Management Impact Agency) guidelines to reduce the amount of waste at its sites and to improve the function of its early warning flood systems. State Minister for the Environment Nabiel Makarim noted that, "it was the first time a court has ruled in favor of the public after several lawsuits on environmental issues that have been filed with the courts."

See: www.goldmanprize.org.

and prospective conflicts over management authority. Several different departments have jurisdiction over similar aspects of marine and coastal affairs (case studies by Husbani; Hardiyanto). These institutions compete for control in order to meet their own departmental targets. For example, the Ministry of Forestry has jurisdiction over conservation areas, the Ministry of Fisheries and Marine Affairs (Departemen Kelautan dan Perikanan/DKP) over fishing licenses and aquaculture, the National Planning Board (BAPPENAS) over real estate development, the Ministry of Mining and Energy over offshore and coastal mining and drilling, and the Ministry of Tourism over recreation and tourist development. Despite the special management needs of sensitive coastal and marine systems, there has been no overarching legislation or coordinated management (case studies by Hardiyanto; Husbani), although currently some drafts are being developed. Furthermore, enforcement of relevant legislation from other sectors is weak in coastal and marine areas, because there is little police presence or monitoring. This has been particularly true for deep-sea fishing.

Although coastal communities may have long established CBPRs to fishing grounds and other coastal and marine resources, these rights are ignored in national legislation. Like forests, marine and coastal resources are subject to the prevailing interpretations of state authority provided under Article 33 of the Constitution and are thereby largely controlled by the state,[36] with locals only allowed limited rights to fish and raise marine species (case studies by Lumintang; Hardiyanto). For example, Article 10 of the Basic Fishing Law requires government licenses for all commercial fishing. These licenses specify the allowable fishing area, require local fishers to obtain licenses to fish within their own territories, and in practice allow commercial fishermen to enter the traditional fishing grounds of local communities (case studies by Sitianapessy; Hardiyanto). This is a further example of the tendency to expand state authority over natural resources and ignore community rights.[37]

As 2002 commenced a draft coastal management law was still being considered. The drafting process has been severely criticized as being top down and too academic and has been stalled. It is likely, however, that that the Ministry of Fisheries and Marine Affairs will assume legal responsibility for issuing fishing licenses, including allowing foreign flag ships to fish in Indonesia's exclusive economic zone (EEZ) and imposing a levy for these licenses (Jakarta Post, July 19, 2001). The ostensible purpose of the new policy would be to crack down on illegal fishing activities by foreign ships. Yet, with minimum patrol and control from the navy, this policy would increase unfair competition and threats to traditional, local community fishing areas.

Another pending policy change is the revocation of anti-trawl regulations covering western Indonesian waters. Trawling has been a big issue in that it creates vertical and horizontal conflicts among fishing constituencies and these conflicts have resulted in the deaths of many poor and artisanal fishermen. Many fishers and NGOs have called for a total ban on trawling in all Indonesian waters. Yet the fisheries ministry seems most interested in maximizing the short-term commercial exploitation of marine and coastal resources exploitation.[38]

Perceptions and Uses of Natural Resources

In summary, the history of Indonesia from colonization to the present day has been characterized by increasing usurpation of CBPRs and the allocation of legal rights to self-interested state actors and allies. The Indonesian state continues to pursue a neo-colonial consolidation of its legal control over natural resources through various tactics, including:

- **Centralization** of authority and simplification of rights,
- **Commodification** of various landscapes and resources, and
- **Criminalization** of local practices and presence in state-claimed resource territories.

Local people, meanwhile, continue to identify different resource zones according to complex arrangements of rights, historical and cultural significance, ecological characteristics, and spiritual and economic uses (case studies by Kanyan; Giay; Jaelani; Laudjeng; Ramlah; Dalip and Priyana). The state, by contrast, invokes a simple dichotomy of either individually owned or unowned land, the latter of which it claims for itself. Further, through its repeated reference to Article 33 of the Constitution, the state claims exclusive rights to allocate and manage most of Indonesia's natural resources. This conventional and widely failing approach is to assert that any devolution of its legal authority is unconstitutional.

Along with complex systems of community-based rights that were simplified, ecological landscapes have also been reduced to commodities. The state has used its authority to classify forests unilaterally by economic "function" without any need for local notification or participation. Populated landscapes and claimed resources with diverse local value have been transformed into objects of resource extraction, whose only official value is as an economic asset.

Local resource uses and livelihoods, however, are not just economic endeavors. They are also political, cultural, religious, and aesthetic acts (case studies by Laudjeng and Ramlah; Kanyan; Giay; Supit). In local perspectives, nature has economic value but is much more than a mere commodity. Community-based resource management activities reflect these different values. Natural landscapes are the stage on which history and personal biographies are played out; they bear the memories and markers of local lives and aspirations. Yet the state's commodification of resources has negated local resource and landscape values and management goals. This approach persists today even under the Reform government, which seems unwilling to question its narrow valuation of natural resources.

The bureaucratization and criminalization of local practice has been especially true in conservation areas and timber production areas where long established villages were relocated, and traditional users of natural resources are threatened with criminal penalties and incarceration. The criminalization of local practice and residence works to further de-legitimate participation by those labeled as "squatters" and "poachers." With this criminalization and the subordination of community-based authority to state institutions, local people have been transformed into demographics (numbers of households, age structures, professions, political affiliations, etc.) and administrative *subjects*, but not into *citizens* with constitutional rights.

While this chapter has examined the abstract evolution of national law and its conflict with local institutions, state policy has real and grave consequences for many local communities. The next chapter draws on case studies to demonstrate the many injustices against local communities that have transpired in various parts of Indonesia as a result of state claims of authority over local institutions and natural resources.

Notes

1. Indonesia's national motto, "Unity in Diversity" (*Bhineka Tunggal Ika*), was invoked during the Suharto regime to promote nationalist sentiment by highlighting Indonesia's local cultural diversity and asserting that it was a fundamental aspect of Indonesian identity. Despite this rhetoric, the regime strove to centralize local governmental administration and ignore local customary legal traditions.

2. Sometimes, as for example with the Philippine Regalian Doctrine, these assertions were based on legal myths and not on legal history. See, e.g., Lynch (1992). The Regalian doctrine was sharply rebuffed by the Philippine Supreme Court in 2000 when it upheld the constitutionality of the Indigenous Peoples Rights Act (Republic Act 8371 of 1997). See Cruz vs. Secretary of Environment and Natural Resources, G.R. No. 13585. The mining industry's petition for reconsideration was denied on 18 September 2001.

3. Hooker (251–253, 1975) describes these courts as expansions of the *Landraad* initially in Java in 1747. They were adjudicated by a bench of local "Regents," whom as "Officers of the King" were under the chairmanship of the European Prefect. Hooker comments that although based on *adat* law, the implementation of this law in these courts was obviously constrained by the degree to which it was "consonant with European ideas." These native courts were established, however, based on the principle of legal pluralism. These courts were later abolished in 1951 after independence, and the state courts given instructions to consider not only statutory law but also unwritten and written *adat* law in deciding cases (Ibid, 279). Indigenous courts were allowed only to adjudicate at the village level.

4. These rights were supported by *Staatsblad* 64/1856, and *Bijbladen* 377 and 2001 (Holleman 1981, 182).

5. A rent, rather than a tax, indicates Raffles' belief in the lack of native ownership (Peluso and Vandergeest, n.d.).

6. Although this well-meaning project of interpreting traditional law may have contributed to the colonial manipulation and use of local community-based institutions (see Burns 1989 for a discussion).

7. Also known as *Agrarishe Wet* 1870. See also Crown Ordinance (*Staatsblad*) 1875, which forbade the foreign ownership of land. This was essentially negated by Crown Ordinance 1885, which made it possible under the Dutch civil code to convert portions of indigenous *adat* CBPRs into private individual titles (Hooker 1975).

8. The first *Domeinverklaring* only applied to directly ruled areas, but it was later expanded to areas of indirect rule in the Outer Islands through the *Domeinverklaring untuk Sumatera* (Article 1, Staatsblad 1874–94f), *Domeinverklaring untuk Menado* (Article 1, Staatsblad 1877–55), and *Domeinverklaring untuk residentie Zuider en Oosterafdeling van Borneo* (Article 1, Staatsblad 1888–58). These later laws were enacted at least partially in response to a desire to grant large long-term leases/concessions for tobacco estates (Potter 1988, 128). Many local community leaders in areas where the tobacco estates were operating signed Short Contracts (*Korte Verklaring*) with the Dutch that brought them under direct rule. This expansion of direct rule occurred either in recognition of the possible revenues from control of valuable oil, timber or other forest products, or as a state effort to consolidate control over territory in order to keep other colonial powers at bay (Furnivall 1944; Irwin 1955).

9. In fact, it was *unnecessary* for there to be any trees in these "forests." They might, as Peluso (1992) points out, be areas that the state desired to be forested, as in restoration projects of degraded land, or areas that outdated or inaccurate maps described as forest where there was none. The key issue in forest classification is defining who is going to have legal rights to land and forest resources within the area. Biophysical characteristics are often of secondary or no importance.

10. This particular vision of "forest functions" later came to be referred to by the Indonesian state as *fungsi hutan*, which continue to be central in management planning.

11.   *Rechtgemeenschappen.*

12. See map for more detailed information on the case study sites.

13. For this reason, where possible the term "local community" rather than "village" is used in this report to minimize confusion between state-imposed and local institutional concepts.

14. Although not legally required to be men, the male-dominated culture of formal administration and the requirements of travel and education have largely discouraged women from holding these positions of leadership.

15. *Pancasila* is the founding ideology of the Indonesian state: belief in one God, national unity, humanitarianism, people's sovereignty, social justice, and prosperity.

16. This was mandated by the Ministry of Interior Regulation No. 2/1981.

17. During September and October 1990, *Operasi Senyum* (Operation Smile) involved military actions to force 6470 people (1735 households) from their homes in the Pulau Panggung Protected Area in South Lampung

and resettle them in a transmigration area of Rawajitu, South Lampung (Fay et al. 1999, 7).

18. In January and February 1995, *Operasi Jagawana* (Operation Forest Ranger) used elephants to destroy 4000 ha of coffee farms and houses and drove 2400 people (474 households) from their homes in Dwikora, Bukit Kemuning and out of the Tangkit Tebak Protected Area in North Lampung.

19. The term *suku terasing* can be variously translated as ethnic groups considered to be "isolated, exotic, deviant, strange, unacculturated, alienated" (Echols and Shadily 1989), words that connote backwardness or primitiveness.

20. See also the 1933 Joint Decree No. 480 by the Ministries of Forestry, Transmigration, Home Affairs, and Agriculture on "forest nomads and destroyers." This decree made no provisions for on-site development of communities but instead proposed to develop them by removing them from their "primitive isolation" and, not coincidentally, away from their valuable resources.

21. Lev (1973), Burns (1989), Li (n.d.), Harwell (2000b).

22. Many Muslim nationalists pressed hard for an Islamic state but were defeated, because the transnational loyalties to Islam and the communities of faithful were seen to be dangerous to the idea of national unity and territorially bounded nationhood. As a compromise, President Sukarno proposed the *Pancasila* ideology that recognized "belief in one God" but did not specify a particular religion.

23. Although *adat* was the philosophical foundation of the new Independent state, European codes that benefited Javanese elite were carried over almost completely intact (Lev 1973).

24. The Basic Agrarian Law is known in Indonesian as *Undang Undang Pokok Agraria,* or UUPA. The law was passed 15 years after Independence was declared.

25. The implementing regulations of the law were never passed. After Suharto seized power, both the law's socialist undertones as well as its association with former President Sukarno were anathema to the New Order state.

26. Strictly speaking, the term *"hak ulayat"* is a term specific to the concept of communal property in Western Sumatra, which is but one component of customary property held by those communities. The term has expanded in usage to mean customary property rights for indigenous communities, including both communal and family inherited property rights. The imprecision of the term has caused some confusion as to the exact nature and scope of *adat* CBPRs.

27. See Articles 3 and 5.

28. The implementing regulations were also never issued for the Law on Population Development and Family Welfare No.10/1992, which guarantees the "right to beneficial use of a territory that constitutes a traditional customary inheritance" (Article 6).

29. Local communities' rights to participation in planning are provided in the Basic Planning Law No 24/1992, Article 5 (Section 1), Article 12 (Section 1).

30. Law on Environmental Management No 4/1982, Articles 5-6; Law on Conservation of Biological Resources and their Ecosystems No 5/1990, Article 4, Article 37 (Section 1); Law on Preservation of the Living Environment No. 23/1997, article 7 paragraph (1).

31. *Penambang Tanpa Ijin* (PETI) or Illegal Miners; *Penebang Liar,* or Illegal (literally, "Wild") Loggers; *Perambah Hutan,* or Forest Destroyers; are all standard terms used by the government to refer to prohibited local practices.

32. Official Explanation of Article 17.

33. One of the implementing regulations for the Forestry Law, PP 6/1999, reinforces the UUPK grant of state power and also admits the presence of indigenous communities and their rights to gather forest products for their subsistence (Article 27, paragraph 1).

34. Official Explanation of Article 18. The UU1/1967 Foreign Investment Law and UU 6/1968 Domestic Investment Law (together with implementing Presidential Instructions (PP) No. 21/1970 on the Right of Forest Enterprises to Harvest Forest Products—later revised by PP No. 18/1975—and PP No. 33/1970 on Forest Planning) further increased the pace of this commercial extraction of resources by clearing the way for capitalization of resource extraction, which had suffered under Sukarno's isolationist/nationalist policies.

35. *Keputusan Mentri Kehutanan* No. 47 /Kpts-II/1998, Article 1, paragraph 2.

36. The Basic Fishing Law No. 9/1985, the Law of Conservation of Biological Diversity and their Ecosystems No. 5/1990.

37. See Zerner (1994) on the use of traditional *sasi* institutions by government officials to control resource access.

38. Personal communication, Nina Dwisasanti, January 2002.

III.

IN THE SHADOW OF THE STATE: NATIONAL LAW AND COMMUNITY-BASED INSTITUTIONS

The legal history of Indonesian natural resource management from the colonial period to the present, as described in the previous chapter, has been one of increasing state authority and the undermining and usurpation of community autonomy and property rights. Local communities have experienced the brunt of official but false distinctions between national and community interests, as well as the state's conflation of commercial extraction, modernity, and "national good."

The Indonesian state has not only claimed to be the sole arbiter of national interest and the exclusive manager of natural resources, but also the ultimate source of law. These assertions, which deny the existence of CBPRs and undermine the capacity of local community institutions, lie at the heart of conflict between resource dependent communities and state policies (Dove 1985). For local communities directly dependent on these natural resources, adverse ecological changes exacerbate their problems and increasingly amount to social as well as natural disasters. Livelihoods are being devastated by the loss of resources crucial to subsistence, as well as invasive pests that ruin agricultural fields.

This chapter adds a field dimension to this report. It draws on cases of community and state conflict throughout Indonesia (see map of case study sites) and highlights some consequences for local institutions of governance and management.[1] The case studies reflect day-to-day realities confronting rural Indonesian citizens. They provide troubling evidence of the persistent tendency of Indonesian national laws and policies to overlook the aspirations, rights, needs, and contributions of natural resource-dependent communities throughout the nation. Whether traditional or migrant, local communities are still largely voiceless in law and policy-making processes that have direct impact on their lives, livelihoods, and rights.

Assertions of state control over community resources ignore the inherent capacity of many local groups to manage natural resources, sometimes more efficiently and sustainably than the state. Despite the debilitating effects of state policy, however, many community-based institutions continue to function. Recent developments in Indonesia, meanwhile, provide the best opportunity in decades to at last secure legal recognition of local community-based institutions and CBPRs.

Factors Influencing Local Community/State Interactions

Despite similar patterns that are evident in state-fostered violations of community rights, not all community/state interactions are identical. Local institutions and practices have been shaped by various influences from states and neighbors (both hostile and friendly), changing markets, and ecological conditions. Safitri[2] observes that differences in effectiveness of local institutions often depend on the

- value and availability of particular resources;
- support or opposition of government institutions;
- levels of intra- and inter-community conflict;
- community faith in and support of local informal and formal leaders, including the degree of democratic representation and accountability in local institutions;
- presence of dispute management mechanisms; and
- experience of local organizing groups.

The character of local community institutions and the trust of their constituencies, the amount of supra-community integration, the rich histories of market, state and social interactions, and physical landscapes intertwine to produce the rich particularities that differentiate the case studies. The cases illustrate that community-based institutions are not static, but are flexible and respond to local needs and developments. They highlight the importance of external influences and underscore the fact that local communities are not isolated but deeply embedded in regional, national, and international networks. Besides economic and social pressures, these external networks include state interventions in local governance and official decisions regarding the use of land and other natural resources. They have prompted many changes in local institutions and resource use. They highlight the need in any sustainable and just community management initiative for dispute management mechanisms, constituent accountability in village governance, and local incentives for conservation. The unique nature of each community's circumstances likewise indicates that diverse legal arrangements will be necessary to address different situations.

Landscapes: Livelihoods and Markets

The most obvious difference among the case studies is their different locales. The ecological landscapes of each community are different, and as a consequence, people in each community have different livelihoods. The presence of particular resources and their economic value can likewise attract the attention of state and business interests, as the cases show.

Some come from marine settings where the resources managed include pelagic and reef fish (sold live, fresh, frozen and salted), corals, clams, sea cucumber, trochus shells, pearls, sea grasses and kelps (case studies by Sitianiapessy; Hardiyanto; Lumintang; Palijama; Mealissa). In coastal zones, people also engage in sago and mangrove management and aquaculture of shrimp and fish, and they also occupy valuable real estate (case studies by Hardiayanto; Giay). In upland forests, communities farm rice and other vegetables; tend fruit, spice, rattan, and rubber orchards; hunt game; and harvest timber, honey, fibers, and resins from forests that are frequently designated as logging concessions or are converted to plantation agriculture (case studies by Dalip and Priyana; Kanyan; Laudjeng and Ramlah; Jaelani; Giay). Hidden below ground are some of the most valuable and most difficult resources to defend against powerful interests coveting oil, gold, silver, tin, coal, bauxite, and marble (case studies by Giay; Supit; Sukanto; Palijama; Sitianiapessy).

The landscapes in which natural resources and communities are located also contribute to how they can be controlled by outsiders.[3] The type, value, and accessibility of natural resources strongly influence the role they have in the lives of local communities, including their vulnerability to outside control. Easy access to coastal and marine resources, for example, has made them more prone to intensive exploitation. Logging, conversion to plantations, and resettlement of transmigrants has heavily impacted forests near navigable rivers or on topography suitable for road building.

Mobility and Relations with Neighbors

Local histories of mobility and relations with neighbors and governments have all etched their influence on community-based natural resource management practices and institutions. Relations with other groups—of kinship, as subjects or rulers, histories of wars and conflict, or seasonal and permanent migrations—have profound influences on memories, claims, and social ties, as well as with wider social groups, which can both cause conflict or strengthen social bonds.

The Benuaq people that live in Desa Benung in the Kutai district of East Kalimantan, for example, are fragments of the larger ethnic group called *Dayak Luangan*, which spreads across many districts. Desa Benung has its origins as a break-off community from a longhouse called Bereg, which then joined with other local communities. The split was caused by a dispute between two families over inherited goods, forest, land, and rivers. The matter was taken to the Sultan of Kutai, who divided rights to the forest, land, and rivers between the different families (case study by Dalip and Priyana). As similar fissions and fusions ensued they expanded ties to people and landscapes and encompassed resources far beyond the bounded administrative unit of *desa*. Relatives, social obligations, and claims to inherited resources that were planted or tended by ancestors, stretch across local maps, confounding the state view of bounded village territories and demographic social units.

Mobility of communities (both voluntary and forced) has also impacted on rights and claims to land and other natural resources. Most inland forest communities moved frequently when their houses became too old or the population increased and closer agricultural fields or bigger houses were needed, or to flee troublesome neighbors or encroaching states (case studies by Dalip and Priyana; Puru Bebe). Sometimes surrounding fruit trees became so large it was feared they would fall on nearby houses. Some local people were forcibly moved to make way for transmigrants or plantations, to resettle them out of what was deemed to be "primitive isolation," or because their residences were arbitrarily located inside of protected or production forests (case studies by Jaelani; Laudjeng and Ramlah; Giay).

Each of these former home sites bears the marks of local management and history: a sign on a tree or a stone marking a particular event or ritual or as a sign of a treaty; an orchard of fruit trees and other useful cultivates planted around a former longhouse where people were born, lived, and died are all evidence of human presence and impact and of shattered expectations of being treated with the respect and fairness that is the birthright of every human being. So too with gravesites or other ritual places. They serve as physical reminders of the ties between the living and the dead and the spirit world. These landscapes carry more than the sustenance and economic resources of the residents; they also carry their memories, inheritance, and aspirations.

Local community rights and autonomy have been profoundly shaped by political environments and histories of relations with various states—whether of colonial, Indonesian, or indigenous origin. The states had various origins, aspirations, and capacities but all left their mark on community institutions and resources. Some relations were brutally exploitative; others were strategic alliances. Some communities took up arms to defend their autonomy; others physically fled external control whenever possible.

One example of cautious alliance with the colonial state was in Minahasa, in northern Sulawesi. In 1679, the Minahasans drove back the Spanish, but the local communities were weakened by the war and threatened by pirate raids and encroachments of nearby sultanates wishing to control trade and extract tributes. The Minahasan states formed an alliance with the Netherlands East Indies Company (VOC) in Ternate on January 10, 1679. It provided them with Dutch military protection in exchange for Dutch access to resources and the freedom to trade. Under this agreement, each side continued to be governed by its own law and retained political autonomy. The Minahasans used this alliance to preserve their independence from other outside powers, without sacrificing their own authority to their Dutch allies. They continued to use this alliance in the struggle for autonomy under the newly formed Indonesian state. Although they were unsuccessful in seceding or establishing a federalist government, to this day, they maintain a strong popular sense of independence from centralized government (case study by Supit).

Moluku had different experiences with Dutch colonial power. Formerly known as "The Spice Islands" for its valuable clove, nutmeg, and cinnamon, Moluku made the Netherlands East Indies the most lucrative colony in the world. As European colonial expansion commenced in the sixteenth century, it was the epicenter of Dutch, especially nutmeg production. Under the VOC, the Dutch regime was oppressive and many lives were lost during massacres, evictions, and other subjugation of the population of the Banda Islands. Local control and management of vital resources was severely hampered.

Following the British Interregnum in 1817, Dutch colonists returned and rebels in Moluku, led by a local leader called Pattimura, stormed a fortress on the island of Saparua, killing the Dutch Resident and his family. The colonial regime sent reinforcements to quash the rebellion, and as a punitive measure, it began felling all local clove and nutmeg

---

Box 2. Treasures of the Forest, Bought with Blood (and How Manhattan Became English)

The forgotten island of Run lies in what used to be known as The Spice Islands, now called Moluku. It is so small that many maps fail to show it, but this was once different. On seventeenth-century copper plate maps, Run is writ large, its size out of proportion to its geography. In those days, Run was one of the most well-known islands in the world, a place of legendary fabulous wealth.

Run's bounty was not derived from gold; nature had bestowed a gift far more precious. A forest of willowy trees fringed the island's mountainous backbone, and trees of exquisite fragrance rose up from its soil. Nutmeg. The seed of the nutmeg tree was a coveted luxury in the seventeenth century—a spice with medicinal properties believed to be so powerful that people would risk their lives to acquire it. Previously prized for its flavor and as a food preservative, nutmeg's price rapidly increased when Elizabethan physicians claimed it was the only cure for the plague, typhoid, and a number of other ailments

(Box continued on next page)

Box 2 (continued)

(such as "bloody flux" and "sweating sickness"), including flatulence and impotence. Nutmeg became more valuable than gold.

Soon, the shipyards of Portugal, Spain, and England were busy with the shipbuilding, in a flurry of activity known as the spice race. It was a desperate and protracted struggle for one of the smallest territories in the world, the Banda Islands. The most coveted of the Bandas and the epicenter of colonial struggle, the tiny island of Run, had an annual harvest of nutmeg large enough to fill a flotilla of ships.

The Portuguese reached the Banda Islands first, in 1511, and were soon followed by the English (Christopher Columbus, sailing for the Spanish, landed in the Americas by mistake). In 1595, the Dutch dispatched their first fleet eastwards with a crew more menacing and warlike than had ever before been encountered in the tropics. Faced with competition from their rivals the English and the Portuguese, the Dutch changed their goal from trade to conquest—conquest of the Banda Islands— and they pursued this with a brutality that shocked even their own countrymen.

This brutality was directed initially towards the local population, which resisted Dutch control. The Dutch made a formal declaration of war against the Banda Islands, who had violently repelled Dutch forces attempting to take the islands by force and to build fortresses there. The Dutch, led by Jan Pieterszn Coen, burned villages and tortured and butchered their inhabitants, decimating the native population from 15,000 to 600 in just a few months.

The Dutch declared that the Bandas would be under Dutch dominion forever and that the local chiefs could only trade with Holland. They then attempted to violently expel the British, which precipitated a bloody sixty-year battle that was to produce the one of the most amazing deals in history: Britain ceded Run to Holland and in return was given the island of Manhattan. The deal was astonishing, not only for its later historical importance, but because it involved an arrangement between two colonial powers to exchange rights and valuable resources on opposite sides of the world—territories that that had been stolen from their rightful owners.

Adapted from:
Milton, Giles. *Nathaniel's Nutmeg*. New York: Penguin Press, 1999.

trees, a tactic that further enforced the Dutch monopoly. In response, local attention turned to protecting valuable forest resources on Saparua, especially through the increased use of institutionalized forest patrols and prohibitions known as *sasi* (although the institution has, according to oral history, been in existence since at least the sixteenth century). The use of *sasi* to patrol marine and coastal resources did not begin until the middle of the twentieth century when reef bombing by Japanese fishing fleets became common (case study by Sitaniapessy. See also Zerner 1994 for more on *sasi*).

In other areas, local religious traditions have attracted state concern and attention. Among fishing communities in Surabaya, East Java, for example, local people have historically been marginalized for their orthodox Islamic beliefs (in comparison to the more moderate *abangan* Muslims), an adherence called *kesantrian*. The Indonesian state fears Islamic orthodoxy as a political force, especially that it might engender more loyalty to religious leaders than to the Indonesian nation. Although geographically close to Jakarta's political center, the East Java region has thus been politically and economically marginalized as a perceived unruly area of state resistance (case study by Hardiyanto). In other areas of Indonesia, people who practice traditional religions are considered by the state to be "not yet religious" (*belum beragama*), that is, not converted to one of the five world religions of Islam, Protestantism, Catholicism, Hinduism, and Buddhism. These people consider themselves religious but at times have been subjected to coercive campaigns of conversion and relocation, ostensibly to order to convert them to more mainstream faiths (case studies by Jaelani; Laudjeng and Ramlah).

The resource-rich yet impoverished province of West Papua (the western portion of the island of New Guinea) has faced similar marginalization. Papua (known by the New Order state as Irian Jaya) was forcibly integrated into Indonesia in 1969. Unlike the rest of the former Dutch East Indies, which were incorporated in the new nation of Indonesia, West Papua remained under Dutch control after Indonesia secured its independence in 1949. The Dutch prepared the territory to become a separate state; in 1961; a West Papuan Council was elected, a national anthem composed, and a flag designed. Despite ethnic and cultural differences and strong local opposition, Indonesia claimed West Papua as part of the Dutch East Indies on the basis of the sanctity of colonial boundaries and declared war against the Dutch over the future of West Papua. In 1963, Indonesia sent troops into the territory. In a brutal military operation to spread fear and intimidation, Indonesia laid the groundwork for a farcical "Act of Free Choice" in 1969 in which 1,026 chiefs loyal to the Indonesian state were selected to vote on the territory's political status under heavy Indonesian military surveillance, a vote which the UN now admits was a farce (Associated Press, November 2001).

Despite its great natural wealth, after more than thirty years of Indonesian subjugation, West Papua remains the poorest province in the country. The indigenous populations have been impoverished through involuntary resettlement away from valuable mining resources located under traditional territories, racial discrimination, economic exploitation (Abrash and Kennedy 2001; Osborne 1985; Tapol 1983), and the non-recognition of *adat* CBPRs (case study by Giay). These sad facts are inextricably linked to unjust local community/state relationships and the value of underground resources.

Local ability to negotiate for legal control over natural resources varies. A stark contrast is provided in the comparison of Lampung West Sumatra and Bali (case study by Safitri). The immigrants of Sumber Agung in Lampung, who came as laborers from Java during the colonial period, are seen by the state as illegal squatters without rights and without any self-governing capacity. Their relations with state forestry officials have been permeated by corruption, distrust, and disenfranchisement. In contrast, many local communities in Bali have had stronger bargaining positions vis-à-vis the state. The communal cooperation necessary for water control in the Balinese system of irrigated rice terraces and Hindu funeral rites is also thought to have produced and sustained strong and resilient local systems of governance that have effectively resistant state incursions (Lansing 1991; Warren 1995). In addition, for centuries the Hindu culture of Bali, as one of the five recognized religions, fit with the New Order vision of culture appropriate to a modern Indonesia. Balinese culture has attracted foreign tourists and scholarly interest, which may have also contributed to its position as a "showcase ethnicity" in the cultural diversity of Indonesia.

As already mentioned, local community/state relations are most frequently associated with the presence of valuable resources, and the struggle for control colors local histories. The strength of state and business claims to natural resources and the territory containing those resources, and the consequent usurpation of local rights and authority, have directly influenced and been influenced by increasing markets for cloves and other spices; luxury and ship timbers (such as teak, ironwood, ramin); precious and semiprecious metals and stones; deposits valuable for industry and energy; salted, frozen, fresh, and ornamental fish and prawns; plywood and paper; oil palm; and most recently, booms in tourism, golf courses and real estate. Far from being isolated, local community histories in the Indonesian archipelago have been steeped in market and state relations since well before the arrival of the Europeans (Wolters 1967; Reid 1993; Lindblad 1988).

Local Leadership

Social relations influence concepts of "community," including who has rights and who participates in management and community decision-making. These relations include intercommunity networks that often determine the degree people outside the community are involved in dispute processing. Some communities have a well-defined nested hierarchy of leadership jurisdictions. For example, in areas of West Kalimantan where Kanyan did his case study, if community leaders (*ketua adat*) cannot satisfactorily mediate a dispute, it is taken to the regional *Temenggung* and then if necessary to the *Patih,* and then to the *Petinggi.* These leaders must be invited to mediate, however, and they have no authority over community life or governance. Other groups, such as the Mentawai of West Sumatra (case study by Jaelani), the Pakava of Central Sulawesi (case study by Laudjeng and Ramlah), and the Tepera, Mooi and Ormu of West Papua (case study by Giay) do not have specific supra-community leadership positions. Instead, consultative bodies made up of leaders from each community (for example, *uma* in West Sumatra, *boya* in Central Sulawesi, and *seray* in West Papua) form and meet when needed, but otherwise have no political or social authority. Rather, they serve as a forum for debate and discussion. Finally, some communities have both consultative bodies as well as a hierarchical leadership structure, where leadership is hereditary. This is true, for example, in Moluku, West Timor, Minahasa, Bali, and some Dayak communities of Kalimantan. These diverse arrangements have structured the relationships between users themselves, as well as between users and the resource, and users and the state.

Most (but not all) local, community-based institutions described in the case studies are based on open debate and participation. Community-based leaders whose power stems from their genealogy or allies rather than from their skills, fairness, or popular support control some traditional institutions. This stratification has been exacerbated by state interventions, especially the virtual appointment of the *kepala desa* (village headman), which created upward accountability to district officials, rather than downward accountability to the community putatively served (see Chapter II).

Types of Conflict

The case studies highlight the sectoral nature of many local level conflicts over natural resources. Different local communities are under pressure from different sectors interested in the exploitation of natural resource extraction sectors, interests that are backed up by state laws and policies. Sometimes different ministries compete not only with local communities, but also with each other, as is evidenced by overlapping concessions that are frequently issued. All of these specificities contribute to unfolding conflicts (and responses) in the field.

Timber[4] and Plantations[5]

A characteristic of state forest management during the New Order was the shifting emphasis from timber extraction to plantations. As valuable timber was extracted from forests, its designated economic "function" was shifted, and it was reclassified from Production Forest to Conversion Forest. If the merchantable timber is depleted (and not replenished), the area is no longer considered by the Ministry of Forests and Estate Crops (MoFEC) to be "productive" forest; frequently the area is then legally designated for plantation agriculture as a means of "rehabilitation."[6] These designations underscore divergent state and local community definitions of productivity and function, as logged forest may still be quite productive for local people and of great use to their livelihoods.

In order to ensure designated areas fulfill their economic "function," local communities have been involuntarily relocated and their CBPRs severed. These relocations are *sometimes* accompanied by compensation, although not for market value of the land and other natural resources that have been usurped.

In a recapitulation of New Order forest policy as experienced by one community, Jaelani[7] recounts a half-century litany of government projects from logging concessions to plantations to protected areas that have relocated and marginalized local Mentawai communities on Pulau Sebirut, West Sumatra. In 1954, the Mentawai were identified by the Social and Cultural Ministry as *suku terasing*—a term that literally means "estranged" or "isolated people," a label intended to indicate a group's backwardness and cultural difference, as "alienated" from modernity. Thus labeled, the Mentawai were forced to abandon their traditional religion and were resettled, ostensibly so they could be organized into modern villages and their lifestyles converted into "modern" ones. The land from which the Mentawai were removed, which was their ancestral territory, was subsequently expropriated by the Ministry and later designated as timber concessions. Leaders of the Mentawai community rejected this expropriation and took the case to court. More than forty years later, in 1997, they finally won and now await enforcement of the decision.[8]

In 1972, after Suharto declared the nation's forests open to foreign and domestic investment[9] for logging and plantations, the entire island of Pulau Sebirut was declared "State Forest" and parceled into four timber concessions. As a consequence, all local communities on the island, regardless of their length of occupancy, were considered to be illegal squatters. All local residence and management practices were deemed crimes punishable by five years in jail and a 20 million rupiah (Rp) fine, or roughly four times the average annual income.[10] In 1994, over 193,000 ha of the island were designated as a National Park,[11] which increased the potential sanctions for living and making livelihoods within the area to ten years in prison and a fine of Rp200 million, or forty times Indonesia's average annual income.[12] But this legal protection apparently did not exclude commercial interests; in 1995 two estate crop companies were given preliminary permits for oil palm plantations on Pulau Sebirut.[13]

Forests have been the sites of military involvement for centuries, but under Suharto the routinized militarization of forest management (Peluso 1993; Peluso and Harwell 2001; Barber and Talbott 2001) was characterized by collusion, violence, intimidation, and bad-faith bargaining to ensure implementation of company projects on community territory.[14] In some cases, playing on these memories of violence became a tactic for intimidation.

Laudjeng and Ramlah describe how Pakava forest territory (in central Sulawesi) has been the stage for violent state activities since the Dutch colonial period. During the early part of the last century, missionaries came and attempted to ban the practice of traditional religion. The Pakava people responded by burning down the church and school. This, in turn, brought violent retaliation from the military that forced residents to acquiesce into nominal conversions. Later the Dutch declared all forest and land in Pakava areas to be state-owned Protected Forest, ostensibly on the basis of slope. Residence was made illegal and communities were relocated, although many soon returned to their original homes. After Independence, the Darul Islam and Indonesian Islamic Army (DI/TII) revolt against the new Indonesian state[15] used remote Pakava forests as their base. Local people still remember the violence and military presence—a fear the Indonesian state has made use of in repeated attempts to intimidate the Pakava in order to control their forest resources.

In 1978, transmigrants from the crowded islands of Java, Bali, and Madura were moved into Pakava territory, and many residents were again relocated under threat of execution by the military. In 1991, an oil palm concession in Pakava territory was allocated to a company in a conglomerate controlled by the Suharto family.[16] The appropriated land was in a swamp forest, rich in sago palms, a valuable survival food for the Pakava. It was also a habitat for wild pigs that, with the size of their habitat reduced, became pests in nearby agricultural fields. Local people were told that Suharto's First Lady, Ibu Tien, was the owner of the concession and that if they resisted, the military would be sent to kill them. The plantation camp and guard posts were reportedly painted with military stripes and camouflage colors and guarded by men wearing uniforms of the elite fighting force known as *Kopassus*—a further effort to use the military and threats of violence to intimidate local residents who might consider disturbing operations in the concession.

Likewise, outsiders have used intimidation and misinformation to arbitrarily impose commercial forestry projects on many Dayak communities (Bachriadi n.d., Fried 2000, Potter 1991). Kanyan reports on one example in Semandang Kiri, West Kalimantan. Based on participatory community mapping, Semandang Kiri has within its community territory 8,894 ha of protected forest, 2,848 ha of agricultural land, 11,200 ha of mixed orchards, and 81 ha of house sites.

More than half of the area, however, has also been designated as State Forest for limited production or conversion forest for plantations. Since 1979 nine HPHs have been established in Semandang Kiri,[17] and now three plantations are planned on the "PIR" (*pola inti rakyat,* or smallholder nucleus estate) model. The PIR model typically requires from each participating household a total of 5 ha of which 2.5 ha is to be worked on by the local household while the remaining 2.5 ha is worked by the plantation (Potter and Lee, 1998). The community must also buy all inputs (fertilizer, seeds, and pesticides) on credit, and its harvest must be sold to a plantation at its prices.[18] The company does not need to purchase land rights, which makes the enterprise less costly for it. Failure to repay loans, however, means forfeiture by the community of its parcels. This results in the plantation acquiring full ownership at little, if any, actual cost. Further, the plantation that owns the factory that processes the fruits can buy the produce at low prices and does not need to pay for any labor on half of its production area (the portion under community management (see Potter and Lee 1997)).

Dalip and Priyana observe that these so-called "community garden" projects provide plantation operators with cheap labor and access to land.[19] The state and some donors that promote these projects have shown a basic lack of understanding of the negative effects on local communities. Smallholder plantations of "improved" rubber varieties in Desa Benung, East Kalimantan require 20 ha of land, which will necessarily come from local community orchards, where each planted rubber tree will be individually owned. Further, the land cannot be intercropped and therefore must be cleared for these new individually owned rubber groves. This shift in ownership and use has caused internal conflicts over project boundaries and beneficiaries. Further, community garden projects require that seedlings, fertilizer, and other inputs be bought on credit, and like the PIR oil palm scheme, community land rights may be seized by project implementers if local debts are not paid in full. According to Dalip and Priyana, similar "community garden" schemes in the area are planned for candlenut, banana, and *pinang*.

Other examples of forest classification that led to the silencing of local participation and the expropriation of local resources are the pulp plantations established in Desa Alas, West Timor. Puru Bebe[20] recounts how, in 1994, 1,110 ha of local forestland were expropriated for plantations without any compensation to local communities. The concessionaires used military intimidation, a biased and corrupt legal system, and a campaign of "development" propaganda and misinformation to coerce the local community into relinquishing their CBPRs.

In July 1994, representatives from the local government and forestry office measured and marked trees Desa Alas without the local communities' knowledge. In January 1995, local officials called a meeting in the village to announce the establishment of the plantation and an accompanying designation of protected forestland. They offered a token compensation of 200 kg of rice and some canned fish. Local residents who complained were told that the community only held use rights to the forest and not ownership rights and that no local community permission or compensation was required. Nevertheless, in December 1997, the Bupati and the head of the provincial forestry office came—flanked by armed military personnel— to obtain community signatures of consent or dissent. Those who agreed were given pens to sign in ink, while those who did not agree were given pencils. The document stated that the community agreed to the establishment of the protected forest, that candlenuts (*kemiri*) may be harvested in perpetuity but other perennials may only be harvested in the first year, and that the number of houses in the protected forest may not increase.

Problems of this sort are not new in West Timor. A provincial office of the National Land Council (BPN) hosted a closed symposium on indigenous territory in 1974. Its solution to the "problem" of traditional lands was articulated in the following reprise of the Domain Declarations:

- All "empty" or "unused" indigenous territory would be considered controlled by the state, and used for community development.
- All indigenous territory already individually owned, in the sense that it had been converted from forest and was continuously and effectively cultivated would be considered owned according to applicable laws.[21]

Conservation and Tourism Development[22]

Conservation initiatives in Indonesia are typically based on the belief that biodiversity conservation (and tourist development) is a "common good" that takes priority over local communities' interests. Although several relevant conservation laws guarantee community participation in decision-making and resource management in protected areas, in practice it is seldom permitted.[23] The designation of areas as legally protected for conservation purposes usually results in their being excluded from human use and habitation. In many cases community access is completely banned. Local communities are expected to bear the entire cost of foregoing the use of protected resources and this is justified as necessary for promoting the greater good of the nation and the world.

Giay[24] describes how the designation of the Cyclops Nature Reserve in Deponsero Utara, West Papua overlapped community territory and enclosed community gardens. In 1978, 225,000 ha were designated as a Nature Reserve,[25] the most legally restrictive category of protected area. Local livelihood activities and residence within the Nature Reserve were banned, and sanctions were put in place for noncompliance. In 1987, new boundaries were drawn that included the villages of Deponsero Utara and their agricultural fields. In 1990, residents petitioned the Worldwide Fund for Nature (WWF) and the World Conservation Union (IUCN) to move the boundaries, which they agreed to do. The provincial Forestry Head, however, denied the petition, stating that it was the provincial government and the Ministry of Forestry that determined forest boundaries, not local communities or international NGOs.

National legislation and state action, in pursuit of commercial gains from tourism dollars, have also prioritized tourism over local well-being, with no concerns for the sometimes unsustainable nature of tourist development and its effect on natural resources. Lumintang[26] describes how the Bunaken National Marine Park in Northern Sulawesi has negatively impacted the local livelihoods of fishing and farming communities, as tourist needs were put ahead of local community needs. In 1991, several islands and surrounding reefs in the area were designated as a National Park.[27] Since that time, local uses, including fishing and farming, have been prohibited, because they are seen as a danger to valuable biodiversity. Meanwhile, tourist boats pollute the water while their anchors and passengers' feet crush and destroy the delicate coral. Hostels, cottages, and restaurants have been built on beachfronts, destroying mangroves, causing erosion and sedimentation, and sometimes even using the coral as construction material for buildings. In addition, many tourists are culturally insensitive and offend local residents with their behavior and dress.

Local community needs in Bunaken were simply overlooked in the single-minded effort to increase income from tourism. This continued even after it became clear that the income would end if the resources tourists came to see were destroyed. Fortunately, recent innovations may turn the tide. Struck by the decline of reefs and fish populations, a divers' association worked with local officials and NGOs to institute a park use fee for divers. The proceeds from this fee will be divided; the central, provincial, *kabupaten,* and municipal governments are to get 5% each, while the remaining 80% is to be returned to communities in the park for conservation activities (NRMP 2000a, 2000b). This is evidence that creative incentives for conservation that more equitably distribute the costs and benefits of resource protection can benefit local communities as well as other interests (see Chapter IV for more evidence).

Mining

The ecological impacts of mining operations include erosion, sedimentation, and pollution of streams; reduced water-holding capacity of soil, degraded vegetation and water tables, reduced wells, reduced areas for farming, and the destruction of valuable trees. The pollution from tailings also adversely impacts fish populations by damaging marine vegetation that provides needed sources of protein. Yet national mining laws are among the most authoritarian, unjust and environmentally unfriendly.[28]

The case studies expose the differences in state and local community views on who holds authority over mining resources. Many local communities consider their CBPRs to extend vertically (i.e., including subsurface resources) as well as horizontally. They do not consider it necessary to ask the government's permission (through permits) to mine on their own territory, although the state tries to discredit these local efforts by calling it "PETI" (Illegal Mining, or *Pertambangan Tanpa Ijin*). Government permits for small-scale mining held by outsiders are considered to be encroachments on local rights.

Article 26 of the Basic Mining Law requires local communities to surrender their CBPRs to mining concessionaires. That same article, however, requires that mining operators notify local communities— a requirement that Supit in Papkelan, Minahasa, North Sulawesi, found to be ignored in practice. The community of Papkelan possesses Dutch colonial documents that legally recognize their rights to protected forests, but mining operators are indifferent. They have begun exploration without any local notification or approval, and without providing any compensation for the negative externalities the local communities will suffer.[29] The response by local people has been to pull up stakes marking the exploration sites.

Similarly, in 1997 mining explorations began in Pulau Nusalaut, Moluku without any local consultation and continued under military intimidation of the community, including implicit threats of violence (given the bloodshed in Moluku at that time) (case study by Sitaniapessy). Likewise, Palijama[30] describes how a mining company[31] in Haruku, Moluku refused to pay fair compensation to the community for lost access to land and other resources. It also unfairly bargained via intimidation by military and government officials and by deliberate tactics to cause internal social conflicts by colluding with some factions in the community.

Sukanto[32] reported that even in provisions for "community mining," the state has disregarded local rights. Following the economic crisis and widespread harvest failures in 1997, many residents in Pondok Natai, West Kalimantan were forced to look for alternative forms of income, including small-scale gold mining. Local residents felt they had rights to mine because they have CBPRs where the operations are taking place. Evidence of their CBPRs includes *tembawang* gardens, housing sites, gravesites, and natural boundaries—all proof that is recognized by surrounding communities. The state, however, has organized its own small-scale "community" mining operations within these traditional territories, but without seeking approval of the community or directly involving them in the mining. This was accomplished through collusion with a corrupt village headman rather than through traditional group discussion and consensus. As a result, aside from mecury poisoning and extreme erosion from water cannons, the mining operations have exacerbated social conflicts.[33]

Marine and Coastal Resources

Coastal and marine ecosystems are fragile and plagued worldwide by accelerating degradation. Highly mobile zones of transition, they cross local and international boundaries and are impacted by practices and policies in effect on all sides. Monitoring and enforcement of coastal and marine laws are notoriously difficult.

One of the biggest threats is from the development of coastlines. Coastal real estate, especially in overcrowded Java, is in itself a valuable commodity, and this sets it apart from the other sectors

---

Box 3. Rio Tinto: Global Operator and Global Compact Violator

Rio Tinto is the largest mining company in the world, with operations on all continents except Antarctica. For years, Rio Tinto's global operations have been beset with controversy, including suppressing trade unions at their Australian operations and exposing workers in a Namibian uranium mine to radiation. The company is accused of negligence and complicity in the civil war in Papua New Guinea, where Conzinc Rio Tinto used to operate a major copper mine.

In an effort to improve its tarnished image, Rio Tinto executives agreed to sign the United Nations Global Compact for corporate responsibility in July 2000. However, despite this effort, there is evidence that Rio Tinto, at its PT Kelian Equatorial mine (PT KEM) in Kalimantan (90% owned by Rio Tinto), has violated Principle 1 ("support and respect the protection of international human rights within their sphere of influence") and Principle 8 ("undertake initiatives to promote greater environmental responsibility") of the Compact.

Last year, the Indonesian government's National Human Rights Commission investigated allegations of abuses at the Kelian mine and found egregious violations. The Commission's report reveals that the Indonesian military and company security have forcibly evicted traditional miners, burned down villages, and arrested and detained protestors since the mine opened in 1992. Local people have systematically lost homes, lands, gardens, fruit trees, forest resources, family graves, and the right to mine for gold in the river, according to the Human Rights Commission. PT KEM employees have also been named in a number

(Box continued on next page)

Box 3 (continued)

of incidents of sexual harassment, rape, and violence against local women between 1987 and 1997. These include abuse and rape committed by senior Australian staff.

Rio Tinto also is accused of environmental abuses affecting the health of the surrounding community. The Kelian mine produces more than 14 tons of gold per year using the cyanide heap-leaching process, which produces contaminated tailings. The tailings are held in a dam and treated in a polishing pond near the Kelian River. Water from the polishing pond pours into the river through an outlet. The company claims that the water is clean, while the community says that people cannot drink or bathe in the water because it causes skin lesions and stomach aches. Locals suffer from skin rashes when they bathe in the river. They can no longer catch the fish they rely upon as a protein source, and the water is alleged to be so contaminated with mine wastes that it is too dangerous to drink.

In 1998, following community demands presented at annual shareholders' meetings in London and Melbourne, PT Kelian agreed to negotiate with a local community organization (LKMTL). Rio Tinto and the Indonesian Forum on the Environment (WALHI) were also parties to this agreement, which was to deal with land compensation, the human rights abuses by mining staff and Indonesian security personnel, pollution, and mine closure plans. The negotiations reached a deadlock in April 2000 when PT Kelian systematically refused to meet community demands for fair compensation for land appropriated by the company for its operations. Then Kelian, after delaying on this issue for two years, reneged the terms of the negotiations with LKMTL by bringing the local district head into the meetings and by opening separate negotiations with a group chosen and backed by him. Unlike LKMTL, which was established through a community meeting of 2000 people, the government-backed team had no mandate from most local residents.

In response, local people and mine workers protested in the spring of 2000 at Rio Tinto's PT Kelian gold mine (as well as similar protests at the Kaltim Prima coal mines in Kalimantan). Hundreds of Dayak villagers blockaded access to the mine, forcing the company to suspend operations. Several community leaders were detained by police for interrogation.

(Box continued on next page)

> **Box 3 (continued)**
>
> The blockades were finally lifted in mid-June of 2000 when mediators intervened. It was agreed that the new group backed by the district head should also be allowed to negotiate, but only on the issue of land compensation. PT Kelian favored this new team led by village officials, who were prepared to settle for much less than the grassroots organization LKMTL. The company's tactic divided the community, and by August LKMTL was forced to accept terms for compensation for land taken for access roads for the mine site, a river port, and land used for company housing. In October 2000, the Indonesian environmental group WALHI issued a strongly-worded statement announcing its withdrawal from the negotiations on the grounds that Rio Tinto had sought to split the community for its own advantage, had misled and insulted LKMTL, and was not genuinely committed to the terms and spirit of the original agreement.
>
> Adapted from:
> Kennedy, Danny. Project Underground. July 13, 2001.
> http://www.corpwatch.org/un/updates/2001/riotinto.html
> *Danny Kennedy is the former Director of Project Underground, a watchdog group that monitors mining and oil industries worldwide. He currently works on Greenpeace's California Global Warming and Energy Campaign.*

because the resources contained rather than the land itself are under contest. Other activities contributing to the destruction of marine and coastal resources include large-scale illegal fishing operations, fishing techniques using explosives and cyanide, coral harvesting, and mining operations. According to the Oceanology Study and Development Centre of the Indonesian Institute of Sciences (LIPI), only 7% of the nation's coral reefs are in good condition, and 70% have been badly damaged.

Coastal communities in Indonesia that rely primarily on traditional fishing methods for their livelihood have been most affected. Since the Suharto era, many communities have tried to end destructive fishing practices and the collusion that makes it possible for powerful interests to violate laws without fear of legal sanctions. Now with a democratically elected government there is greater hope for reform.

Local fishing communities have formed new associations, such as the anti-trawl network and GRANAT. They have teamed up with NGOs to press their demands. In cases where there has been little response or official support, they have taken unilateral action. In Kumai, Central Kalimantan, villagers burned a Thai-owned boat in protest against the lack of effective police action against illegal fishing.

As in other sectors, CBPRs to marine and coastal resources are not recognized. Existing laws and policies, including those establishing the new Ministry of Marine Affairs, emphasize modernization (or capitalization of commercial extractive activities) and licensing. This has led to similar patterns of collusion and "rent-seeking" behavior by government officials and commercial entrepreneurs. In deep-sea fishing, this emphasis is exacerbated by even weaker enforcement than in the forest and mining sectors, as there is no police enforcement. Sitaniapessy[34] provides a case in point in Pulau Nusalaut, Moluku where pelagic fishing licenses over traditional fishing areas were granted to large ships. This resulted in the devastation of fish stocks and local livelihoods in these areas. At the same time, the state requires local fishers to have licenses to fish in their own traditional territories.

A more chilling example comes from the Laalo community of the Bangkurung Islands of Central Sulawesi (case study by Jamalludin; see also Lowe, 2000). Dependent on fishing, the Laalo have long been troubled by the degradation of reefs and fisheries caused by cyanide and dynamite fishing in their community area (case study by Jamalludin). These activities are protected by the local military and police, are paid for by commercial fishing vessels (many illegally entering Indonesia's waters) and are carried out by neighboring community members. Fish caught with these destructive methods are then sold to large fishing fleets. The primary target of the cyanide fishers is the valuable Napoleon Wrasse, which is sold live to restaurants and fish markets as far as Japan and Hong Kong. When Laalo leaders attempted to address the problem by inviting local parliamentarians and police officials from a neighboring police district, community members were threatened and intimidated by the local police force.

Hardiyanto[35] illustrates how real estate development has disadvantaged coastal fishing communities like the Kedung Cowek in Surabaya, East Java. The Kedung Cowek case is a reflection of the greater failure of the New Order policy to live up to the mandates of protecting and managing natural resources for the maximum prosperity of the people.

Existing legislation on coastal planning requires public participation and environmental impact assessments (EIA) before development can legally occur.[36] It also requires that development be undertaken in a way that benefits the community as a whole, while protecting natural resources.[37]

Yet in Kedung Cowek, these requirements and objectives have not been met. Municipal plans to develop the eastern shore of Surabaya for expensive homes and hotels and to build a Surabaya-Madura bridge have meant that the development of surrounding coastal zones only benefits urban elites and not resource-dependent coastal populations.

Centralized planning proceeded without local consultation or review, or an Environmental Impact Assessment (EIA). Ensuing developments have decreased areas available for local fishing, and increased water pollution and sedimentation that has depressed fish yields. Mangrove stands designated for conservation—with biodiversity and fish habitat values as well as public value as reducers of salt-water intrusions and flooding—have been completely destroyed in many locales.

Adverse Impacts of State-Controlled Resource Management

From environmental and human rights perspectives, the legacies of the New Order state's laws and policies encourage unbridled commercial extraction of Indonesia's natural resources. Nearly 50 million ha of Indonesia's forest have been lost since the 1950s (World Bank 2000a). Over 8 million ha were burned in the widespread fires of 1982 and 1997–98, fires prompted by laws and policies that favor plantations over local community welfare, fires that pumped millions of tons of carbon into the atmosphere[38] and created a plume of choking smoke and ash that stretched to mainland Southeast Asia.[39]

The fires provide vivid illustration of the widespread, adverse impacts that overly centralized natural resource laws and policies can have. Continued official support for large-scale clearing of forests for plantations likewise ensures that the phenomenon will be repeated. Huge areas of piled and dried vegetation are set afire all at once and easily spread into nearby forests or community gardens, especially during the dry climate conditions in which much burning is done.[40] Drier forest microclimates in logged areas further increase fire hazard. The chronic social conflicts between local communities and concessionaires create apathy (if not animosity) and reduce incentives to fight fires in areas that have been removed from local control. This friction makes fire a weapon frequently used by both sides to stake claims or wage revenge (Tomich et al. 1998).

In addition to species and habitat loss from fires and deforestation, soil loss from logging, plantation estates, and mining have impoverished ecosystems and sedimented rivers and coastlines, causing plumes of muddy sediment to spill out into the ocean. Soils are compacted, thereby reducing water-holding capacities and eroding water tables. Rivers are clogged with loose timber and polluted with mining tailings and chemical log preservatives. Mangroves have been destroyed for beachfront access, resulting in biodiversity loss, salt water intrusions, erosion of coastlines, and flooding. Sensitive and biologically diverse coral reefs have been devastated by tourists' anchors and feet, chemical pollutants, and algal growth.

With nearly 75% of Indonesia's land area (143 million ha of 190 million ha total) allocated to forest concessions (World Bank 2000b), and a surfeit of permits for commercial fishing trawlers and coastal tourism, little legally remains under the current framework for community forestry, farming, and fishing.[41] The collusion between big business and government has forced many local peoples to surrender their CBPRs to business operations. This has frequently taken place under military or police intimidation and campaigns of misinformation and unfair bargaining. In addition, collusion has spread to unaccountable village officials. Concessionaires oftentimes intentionally promote social conflict as a deliberate tactic to destabilize community unity and opposition by targeting some factions of the community (typically the *kepala desa* and his officers) to obtain unilateral "permission" to go forward with controversial projects.

Violations of basic due process, and the lack of just compensation and fair wages and labor relations, have resulted in widespread injustices and a worsening ecological crisis. They have also generated deep distrust of regional (and district) bureaucrats and business operators—frustration that has in many places boiled over into violent confrontation in which logging and plantation camps have been burned and had estate trees felled, or have been reoccupied (known in Indonesia as *rekleiming*).[42]

Finally, the debilitating effect of village administration law on local institutions is clear. While local adat institutions have undergone many changes over the decades, many remain legitimate and relevant centers of authority and decision-making. The case studies and other field research vividly demonstrate that parallel forms of community-based leadership are alive and active at local levels throughout Indonesia.

As with adat CBPRs, however, local community-based institutions are legally unrecognized and have long been under relentless attack. They are in constant danger of being disregarded and undermined by outsiders. But since 1997, the promise of a budding democracy and a return to constitutionality may yet turn the tide in favor of respect for and legal recognition of CBPRs. This would be a major contribution towards effectively promoting national reconciliation.

Local Community-Based Management Capacities

Besides the harm that Indonesian laws and policies inflict on local communities and ecosystems, their implementation is often inefficient. Government programs that ignore or deny the local governance and resource management capacities, and instead impose uniform state-centric management regulations, are based on incomplete information. However well-intentioned, most existing state laws and policies fail to allow for variations in local capacities and environments, and as a result are locally inappropriate and ineffective (case studies by Lumintang; Sukanto; Giay). The explosion of international interest in "local knowledge" and "indigenous technical knowledge" highlights the growing realization that community-held social and ecological information about fish and game behavior and reproduction, fruiting and flowering of trees, and so forth can make an important contribution to sustainable natural resource management (Geertz 1983; Alcorn 1981; Altieri 1989; Brush and Stabinsky 1996).

A frequently unacknowledged advantage of community-based management systems, especially those maintained by long-term users, is the in-depth information they possess. Conventional resource economists and game theorists have tended to view local resource users as atomized individuals who make decisions seemingly without

73

knowing or caring about their neighbors. But more innovative and insightful research now demonstrates otherwise (Rose 1994; Runge 1986; see also http://www.indiana.edu/~iascp). Members of small, cohesive communities are increasingly understood to be far from anonymous and isolated. Instead, they have daily contact in a number of different arenas and have individual rights that are balanced by responsibility to a larger local community.[43]

The maintenance of social networks through local norms of reciprocity is important in controlling access to diverse and environmentally important "resources" (e.g., shared labor during harvest periods or during household crisis, networks for access to wage labor opportunities or trade of various goods, and participation in important rituals such as funeral rites, among others). Reputation, in this context, can be a powerful motivational tool for following rules (case studies by Hardiyanto; Maelissa; Sitianispessy). This pressure, which includes not only the social sphere of the local community but also relations with the spiritual world, is translated in many communities into a view of the balance of rights with responsibilities.[44] The strength of local suasion to follow rules, as well as proximity to natural resources, are other potent reasons for recognizing the capacities of local, community-based natural resource management institutions.

Many community-based legal and ritual principles also reflect an understanding of the wider consequences of human action, a central tenet in many forms of community-based management. This emphasis on responsibility mitigates some individual behavior that might otherwise cause adverse environmental impacts or social disharmony (case study by Sukanto). In many local communities, proper rituals to seek the permission of spirits are required before farming and, in some cases, before logging, fishing, or gathering particular forest or marine products. These local notions of consequence hold not only for management activities but also for still unresolved offenses in the social sphere. Under traditional laws, ritual fines are incurred—not as compensation or revenge—but as cleansing of cosmic and social disharmony. Neglect of these rituals is traditionally believed to threaten the entire community with displeasure of the spirits in the form of pestilence, epidemics, climatic extremes, accidents, and deaths.[45]

Drawing on local idioms of human misbehavior and their costs, many local people believe that the greedy and unjust behavior of concessionaires, politicians, and law enforcement officers involved in the conversion of forest to commercial timber enterprises and plantations that has caused the ecological and social dysfunctions plaguing Indonesia's countryside (Harwell 2000a). The recent post–New Order state's recognition of governmental responsibility for the destruction of natural resources and the undermining of local welfare is yet another confirmation of this belief, and requires that a new approach to natural resource laws, policies and management be developed and implemented. This will entail, first and foremost, a renunciation of the state claim to exclusive legal control over much of Indonesia's natural resources and territories, and legal recognition of *adat* CBPRs and local institutions of governance.[46]

The durability of customary legal systems, or *hukum adat*, throughout Indonesia reflects the enduring strength of local community-based authorities. These authorities are legitimated through everyday interactions between individuals and communities, present generations and ancestors and the spirit world, as well as between humans and nature. This is not to suggest a static or isolated character to *adat* law, but rather to emphasize its local relevance. Locally significant concepts of rights and obligations draw on this sense of integration and balance and also prioritize local community interests, including environmental interests. Local norms are often more acceptable than those imposed by distant and uninformed outsiders who have other interests in mind. Local, community-based institutions, therefore, can often provide the moral legitimacy and required persuasion to abide by rules that external authorities lack.

A final common and important characteristic of local community-based management is low implementation costs—a characteristic that makes them more economically efficient than many government sponsored and donor supported approaches. All management schemes have costs—drawing up rules, contacting relevant parties, patrolling to catch offenders, adjudication for disputes, levying punishment, and so forth (Rose 1994). In addition, there are costs of failure and resultant overuse of the resource caused by externalities associated with all imperfect management schemes. By using local community-based institutions, some costs are avoided altogether (e.g., identifying and contacting users, disseminating information about new rules, setting up regulatory bodies); others are passed on to the beneficiaries themselves, thus internalizing such costs (e.g., policing and enforcement). In addition, the costs of potential failure are reduced by the ease with which local people can police themselves, because they are familiar with the environment and the users involved and in general are more in number and live on-site much more than outside regulatory agents. Further, it is in the users' own self-interest to catch offenders and contribute to an even more efficient enforcement system.

Nevertheless, the most compelling arguments for community-based control of natural resources, and those with which this report is concerned, are more fundamental than the potential for local institutions to be more cost-efficient and effective at protecting resources. They are based on the principles of social justice, humanitarianism, and democracy—principles found in the spirit of the Indonesian Constitution but abandoned in the New Order state's policies and practices.

The cases relied on in this chapter illustrate that in promulgating and enforcing national laws that support its consolidation of power and control, the state has consistently violated community rights, including:

- Community-based property rights;
- Community right to self-government through local *adat* institutions, as provided for by Article 18 of the Constitution;
- · Rights to participate in natural resource planning, including the legally required consent of entire communities (not just their formal headmen) in surrendering rights to business operations;[47]
- Rights to life and livelihoods, including a healthy environment;
- Rights to due process, including fair bargaining and just compensation during state assertions of eminent domain; and
- Rights to equal treatment before the law.

The ongoing violation of these rights fosters coercion and bad-faith bargaining and contributes to Indonesia's worsening environmental problems. It reflects the arbitrary subordination of local needs and welfare to external considerations, especially large-scale commercial concerns. It also undermines local community support for the Indonesian nation. Local community efforts to forge agreements with regional governments and commercial operations are increasing, however, and some are described in the next chapter.

These initiatives may yet signal a return to popular sovereignty as guaranteed under Indonesia's Constitution.

Notes

1. In this report, institutions are understood to mean any set of formal and informal rules that mediate human relations, with each other, with nature, and with the spiritual world (Agrawal 1997). Enclosed within sovereign states, there are many diverse communities that both develop and enforce their own rules for behavior through these institutions and without reference to, or in spite of, formal state-centric legal structures.

2. Program Penelitian dan Pengembangan Antropologi-Ekologi, Universitas Indonesia, Depok.

3. Husbani discusses international aspects of marine and coastal resource management.

4. For other examples of conflict between logging operations and communities, see also Bengici of West Kalimantan and HPH PT AK (Kalimantan Review No. 38/VII, 1998, 16–17); the Wooi and Mee of Nabire, West Papua against the HPH PT PY and the Oyehe against HPH PT PTYU (Patay and Saway 1993).

5. For other examples of conflicts between communities and plantations, see also the cases of the Yamdena of Moluku against HPHTI PT Inhutani I, PT MA and PT ANS (Dietz 1996); the Jangkang Dayak of West Kalimantan against HPHTI PT InFT (Mayer 1996); the Benuaq Dayak of East Kalimantan against the Oil Palm plantation PT London Sumatra (personal communication with Longgena Ginting, coordinator of SKUMA (Solidaritas Aksi untuk Masyarakat Adat) 1999); and multiple village complaints against plantation companies PT SML and PT AS in Lampung (WWF-WARSI 1999). Also see the now famous case of the Bentian Dayak of East Kalimantan, who took to court their protests against the HPHTI PT MH, PT Inhutani I and PT TD, owned by timber baron Bob Hasan. Traditional Bentian leader Loir Botor Dingit received the prestigious Goldman Environmental Prize in 1997 for his leadership of community protests, as described in Chapter V.

6. Potter and Lee (1998) document that this change of forest classification status involves an unwieldy amount of bureaucratic red tape, such that shady deals are frequently made to declare unlogged forest to be "critical land," thereby releasing any restrictions of selective logging that normally hold on logging concessions, and allowing the clear cut of the contracted area. The sales of these logs together with favorable lending rates are

where most concessions make their money, not through the production of pulp or palm oil. Barr (1998) shows that in recent years the amount of wood originating from timber concessions is decreasing, while timber from plantation clearing permits is increasing.

7. Lembaga Riset dan Advokasi Padang, West Sumatra.

8. Putusan Pengadilan Negri Padang 39/Pdt/G/1997.PN.Pdg.

9. UU 1/1967 on foreign investment and UU 6/1968 on domestic investment.

10. pp. 28, 1985: Article 6, paragraph 1; Article 9, paragraph 2; Article 18, paragraph 2.

11. SK Menhut 407/KPTS-II/1993.

12. UU 5/1990 article 33; article 40, paragraph 1.

13. SK Gubenor SumBar 525.26/2003/perek-1995.

14. This tactic of fostering an atmosphere of violence has gone terribly wrong in Kalimantan, where the portrayal of these areas as centers of primitive violence and disorderliness has, at least in part, contributed to recent outbreaks of brutality (see Peluso and Harwell 2001).

15. Orthodox Muslims who wanted Indonesia to be an Islamic Muslim state, bound by Islamic Law, led the revolt.

16. PT.Pasangkayu of the Astra Group.

17. PT.Dayak Besar, PT.Hutan Raya, PT.Erna Djuliawati, PT. Inyuitas, PT.Sumber Jaya Baru Utama, PT.Kawedar, PT.Inhutani II, PT.Yunan dan PT.Kayu Mukti.

18. Oil palm fruits quickly rot and so cannot be stored until a favorable price is offered.

19. Komite Hak Asasi Manusia & Lembaga Bina Benua Puti Jaji, Samarinda East Kalimantan.

20. Yayasan Konsultasi dan Bantuan Hukum "Justitia," Kupang, West Timor.

21. This "consensus" was made legal through Peraturan Daerah Tingkat I NTT No. 8/1974 (entitled "implementation, investigation and resolution of traditional land problems in NTT"). PerDa No. 8/ 1974 Article 2, paragraph (1) states that "land formerly held by traditional communities is considered as land under the authority of the local government c.q. Gubernur Kepala Daerah."

22. The sub-bureau of Nature Protection (KSDA) within the Ministry of Forestry and Estate Crops, regardless of whether the protected area is forestland or marine, administers protected areas. This has created several legal inconsistencies, as discussed in Chapter 2. For other examples of conflicts over designated conservation areas, see the cases of the Katu of

Central Sulawesi and Lore Lindu National Park (*Down to Earth* No. 36, 1998); the Moronene of Southern Sulawesi and Rawa Ope Watumohai NP (Bediona et al. 1999), which was particularly egregious including the reported armed attack and shooting of protestors, burning of villages and their orchards, and the arbitrary detention of twelve protestors (Bediona in Sirait et al. n.d). For other examples of conflicts with state "protected forest" (on the basis of slope, soil, and rainfall indices), see the Peminggir of Lampung (Kusworo in BSP, 1999).

23. In addition to the Nature Reserve, mining explorations have been conducted in the area without any community notification or consent.

24. Lembaga Pengajian dan Pemberdayaan Masyarakat Adat, Jayapura, Irian Jaya.

25. SK Menhut 365/KPTS-II/1987.

26. Yayasan Suara Nurani, Tomohon, North Sulawesi.

27. SK Menhut 730/KPTS-II/1991 and 96/KPTS-II/1993.

28. Abrash and Kennedy (2001) note that in Papua "Freeport and other U.S. commercial interests in Indonesia's natural resources, low-wage labor and lax regulatory regime have dominated U.S. policy towards Indonesia. This influence has blocked effective U.S. policy approaches to address the Indonesian government's repressive practices and policies."

See www.mpi.org.au/indon/eng_moving_mountains.html.

29. PT. Soputan Meares Mining.

30. Lembaga Pengajian Hukum dan Masyarakat.

31. PT. Aneka Tambang.

32. Yayasan Triu Keadilan, Ketapang, West Kalimantan.

33. Traditional communities in West Kalimantan also believe that miners must observe proper ritual propitiations—a form of asking for "permission"—from the spirits, not from government officials. They believe that it is the spirits who hold ultimate authority to approve of management decisions.

34. Yayasan Baleo-Moluku.

35. Lembaga Bantuan Hukum Semarang, East Java.

36. For public participation see UU 24/1992 Basic Planning Law Article 22, Section 5; for EIA requirements see UU 23/1997, PP 51/1993.

37. UU 24/1992 Planning Law Article 10, Section 3, Line b, c. See also UU 4/1982 on Conservation and UUPLH 23/1997 on Environmental Management.

38. Indonesia's 1997 forest fires and burning peat soils, which can smolder underground for years, have been estimated to have released almost a billion metric tons of carbon in to the atmosphere—an amount estimated

to be greater than that emitted by all the power stations and automobiles in Western Europe over an entire year. (*New Scientist*, October 1997).

39. This trans-boundary disaster brought sharp criticism from international observers and even from the historically non-interventionist governments of the Association of South East Asian Nations (ASEAN). See Harwell (2000a) for a discussion of the diverse interpretations of the fires disaster of 1997 and their myriad implications.

40. Most of the fires during 1997–98 were in plantation concessions and previously many were in logged over concessions (Mackie 1984; Leighton and Wirawan 1986; Gellert 1998).

41. It is estimated that only between 92 and 112 million ha of this State Forest remains forested, but under prevailing legal interpretations the classification of forest land nevertheless perpetuates ongoing state control over these areas (World Bank 2000b).

42. See full report, as well as *The Guardian*, 20 July 1998; *International Markets Insight Reports*, 21 October 1998; *Jakarta Post*, 6 February 2001.

43. Ostrom (1994) calls this local capacity for cooperation "social capital," which is "created when individuals learn to trust one another so that they are able to make credible commitments and rely on generalized forms of reciprocity rather than on narrow sequences of *quid pro quo* relationships." See also Scott (1976) for discussions of peasant moral economy.

44. These ideas of rights bearing responsibility are not so exotic—they are precursors to the "polluter pays" and "intergenerational equity" concepts now widely accepted in various international environmental agreements, as argued by Husbani. It is also true that nowhere—even in the "modern" capitalist concept of individual freehold title—are rights possible without reciprocal responsibilities, except under the most extreme totalitarian coercion. If non-rights holders do not agree to their responsibilities to respect the rights of the rights holders, those rights will be meaningless. See Hohfeld (1913, 1917).

45. See also e.g., Dove and Kammen (1997); Dove (1998); Harwell (2000a); Alcorn (1981, 1990) for more discussions of indigenous concepts of human-nature linkages and their consequences.

46. While there has been recognition from some members of the government that concessionaires (rather than swidden agriculturalists, as claimed in the past) were predominantly responsible for the widespread fires of 1997–1998, this was primarily due to overwhelming evidence from satellite photos and subsequent international attention and pressure. It is worth noting, however, that the government response was far from unified.

The Ministry of Environment made public the GIS coordinates of plantation concessions. See Harwell (2000a) for a detailed discussion of the interpretation of the fires disaster.

47. Basic Planning Law No. 24/1992, Article 5 (Section 1), Article 12 (Section 1).

IV.

LOCAL INITIATIVES AS PRECEDENTS FOR RECOGNITION OF COMMUNITY RIGHTS

With the ferment in Jakarta about key leadership changes and the drafting of new national legislation, it might be easy to overlook other important evidence of change that is taking place at local levels. Throughout Indonesia, local communities and their advocates are not waiting for legal and policy reforms. Rather, they are taking advantage of this transitional period of *reformasi* to press for and to create reforms on their own terms and in their own areas.

Although many who benefit from the status quo resist reform, they have often been unable to control local developments. In many regions and districts, local communities are negotiating for—and in some cases have already successfully won—legal recognition of their community-based property rights (CBPRs). This has taken place by way of agreements with officials of local governments, forest and protected-area officials, and even from some logging and plantation companies. Indonesian university scholars and NGO partners of the Biodiversity Support Program's (BSP) KEMALA project have mediated some of these agreements. Most of the information in this chapter is taken from the BSP KEMALA Technical Reports from 1999–2001. These reports provide concrete evidence of fundamental changes that are already underway. Some are precedents that can inform future law, policies, and programs for legal recognition or grant of CBPRs.

Local Government Recognition of CBPRs and Local Management Practices

The National Land Board (BPN) has reiterated its priority to allocate land rights to local communities, including those within national forest zones. This decision was made in September 2000 in the BPN's final report on Land Policy Reform under the Land Administration Project pursuant to Agrarian Ministry Decree (PerMen BPN) No. 5/1999. The identification and community mapping of areas under *adat* management (*wilayah adat*) is proceeding in West and East Kalimantan, among other places.

In West Kalimantan, *adat* management areas are to be put under the authority of community-based institutions, headed by traditional village representatives from among the indigenous groups living in the areas and adjacent territories. Traditional areas serving as test cases include those of Dayak Kenayatn in Pontianak; and Dayak Mayau, Mualang, and Katungau in Sanggau; and Dayak Jelai in Ketapang. These areas were picked on the basis of availability of community maps, analyses of land uses, existing conservation and land management agreements between villages, and the strength of local institutions. *Lembaga Bela Banua Talino* (LBBT), a public interest law NGO in Pontianak developed a draft local regulation on village governance. The Sanggau district legislature is expected to move ahead on a village governance law to redefine villages in more locally appropriate ways that also cover non-*adat* or mixed communities. The local office of the NGO Pancur Kasih in Sanggau is actively working with the local legislature while completing the mapping of Dayak Mayau villages.

In East Kalimantan, *SHK-Kaltim* has initiated discussions with the West Kutai District Head and District Spatial Planning Office. Its members have given testimony to the Kutai Induk District Assembly (DPRD) concerning the establishment of village legislatures and the incorporation of community maps and land-use plans into district land-use plans. Discussions have included the need for a mechanism for legally recognizing and registering CBPRs.

SHK-Kaltim has also supported communities in seven villages in Kedung Pahu Hulu and Idaatn watersheds. This includes helping establish village legislatures and restructure village governments to be more transparent, accountable, and democratic. Legislative members from some of these communities presented and discussed their experiences with the district head and other district officials in a two-day workshop organized by *SHK-Kaltim*. They secured a commitment from the district head to issue a decree that legitimates their efforts and establishes them as a pilot case for the creation of community legislatures in the district. *SHK-Kaltim* also helped to develop a draft model district regulation on village governance to be presented to the District Assembly after it was formed in February 2001.

SHK-Kaltim organized two workshops that brought together local governments, community leaders, and NGOs to discuss experiences in Kedung Pahu with establishing village legislatures and village land-use maps and plans, and on the techniques and processes of participatory mapping. It has helped to draft and advocate for specific district regulations to incorporate community land-use plans into West Kutai district land-use plans, as well as for formal legal recognition and registration of customary CBPRs. *SHK-Kaltim* has also drafted terms of reference for a provincial coalition of NGOs. This included helping to organize a series of three workshops aimed at defining and reaching agreement on the roles and responsibilities of village, district, provincial, and national governments.

Recognition of Community Land-Use Systems in Spatial Plans

There are twelve sub-districts in West Kalimantan that have recognized community land-use systems: Simpang Hulu, Sekadau Hilir, Sengah Temila, Menjalin, Sungai Laur, Bonti, Belitang Hilir, Sandai, Kapuas Hulu, Mandor, Toho, and Jelai Hulu.[1] In the process of gaining a semblance of legal recognition of their CBPRs, strong community-based institutions ensured a collaborative process to develop and implement the village level land-use plans. Villagers found local sanctions to be more effective in areas where there are strong *adat* institutions. The regional autonomy law reinforces this.

In villages with weaker community-based institutions, recognition and adherence to land-use plans is more problematic, even if the sub-district government is supportive. For example, when villagers in Lintang, Sanggau wanted to impose *adat* sanctions over a Dayak who illegally extracted resources, the latter refused to obey and sought sub-district government intervention. The sub-district would not intervene, and the problem went unsolved.

The Jayapura's District Planning Agency in Papua and the local legislature have used community maps in regional spatial planning.[2] As a result, the spatial plans have constrained intensive encroachment of oil palm and gold mining "community cooperatives" (*Kopermas*) on ancestral domains that have been unilaterally initiated by the Ministries of Cooperatives, Agriculture, Forestry and Estate Crops, and Mining and Energy.

YBAW, with assistance from LPPMA, WWF-Sahul, *Konpenma*, and YPLHC are now compiling results of community discussions at the three confederations in Baliem Valley to obtain legal recognition of CBPRs by the local government. They hope for a district regulation to recognize the CBPRs of confederations of *adat* communities in Walesi, Ibele, and Heatnem.

Incorporation of Village Maps into Sub-Districts[3]

In May 2000, the village heads (*Kepala Desa*) of Pulan, Ungak, Apan, Sungai Tebelian, and Sungai Utik, all within the sub-district of Embaloh Hulu, Province of West Kalimantan formalized recognition of village initiatives in land and resource management, and this improved environmental conditions. The village heads met with the district legislature (DPRD) to determine the needs for recognition of CBPRs and management authority in a local regulation on village government. The representatives of this area joined with other village representatives in Silat Hulu to show the government ways in which village maps can be used to develop an overall land-use plan for the entire district.

The villagers have shown insight and innovation by using the opportunity provided by government recognition to also make some positive changes to protect valuable resources. Land uses generally include rubber orchards, limited-use forests, rice fields, and enriched forest fallows, protected *adat* forests, and mixed-forest gardens *(tembawang)*. Recognition for the villages meant allowing them to pursue current land uses, including the regulation of extractive enterprises. Trading of rubber and timber is an important part of their local economies. Recent local research, however, showed that the harvesting of timber was increasingly unsustainable and was partly in response to uncertain income from rubber due to unstable prices.[4] With government recognition, villagers in the sub-district of Embaloh Hulu have responded by imposing *adat* regulations over more areas. They have also agreed to set aside forest reserves in four villages and to regulate cutting in the limited-use forests. Villagers hope to maintain a higher rubber quality that will command higher prices, and they have assigned *adat* leaders to implement this policy across the five villages through mapping and management planning.

In the sub-district Silat Hulu, the villages of Selangkai, Riam Tapang, and Bangan Baru have mapped their territories and submitted this information to the sub-district and local legislature for recognition and use in local spatial planning. The communities of Silat Hulu employ similar management practices as those of Embaloh Hulu (see above). An *adat* institution is charged with the regulation and enforcement of rules on protection and exploitation of natural resources, and it involves some local units of government as well.

The formal recognition of local maps and CBPRs immediately proved advantageous to local communities and generated good will towards the government. Villagers found the maps to be an especially useful tool for resolving disputes with logging concessions in the area (PT Alas Kusuma and PT Duta Hendra Mulya), including compensation for destroyed *tengkawang* trees, honey trees, and rattan gardens. Using the maps, compensation was based on the

---

Box 4. Community Mapping: Protecting CBPRs and Local Cultures

The Dayak people are indigenous to Kalimantan and have their own *adat* rules, institutions, and sustainable natural resource management systems. Yet, like many natural resource dependent communities around the world, they are legally marginalized. Their indigenous rights have been subordinated by the state, often to powerful business interests that constantly encroach on their ancestral domains. The Dayak, however, are beginning to recognize the power of community mapping to protect their CBPRs from intruders and to manage their unique way of life.

Mapping has long been used as a tool by state authorities to increase control over space, to define territories, and to demarcate boundaries. Forest mapping in particular has long had a controversial history. Despite the large number of indigenous people living in or around forests,

(Box continued on next page)

Box 4 (continued)

these areas are routinely gazzetted as state-owned. Transferring mapping technologies to local communities empowers them to articulate and define their perception of their CBPRs and natural resource management systems.

By combining locally generated sketch maps with government base maps, and using GPS technology to check for accuracy, Dayak villagers create legally cognizable evidence and proof of their occupancy and CBPRs. Community mapping has additional benefits. It demarcates and helps protect and preserve traditional territories and knowledge. It increases local community capacities to deal with external impacts. It can also help to resolve local disputes over natural resources and to create new opportunities for local participation in land-use planning and conservation.

Community mapping by gender also provides women, whose opinions are often overlooked, a means to articulate their needs and to play a more active role in planning processes. During Dayak mapping exercises, women stressed the need for forest conservation to protect natural resources, while men stressed the importance of hunting and economic land uses. By combining these diverse perspectives, community mapping can help indigenous and other local communities gain legal recognition of their CBPRs and natural resource management systems.

Challenges to Mapping

In many cases, mapping community boundaries poses formidable challenges. There are often layered historical claims to territories in Indonesia, where many communities have been highly mobile, both voluntarily and under state coercion. In addition, the New Order redefinition of administrative village (*desa*) boundaries, supported by local officials' attempts to assert their territorial control, has compromised the ability of many local communities to defend their traditional CBPRs to natural resources against other, sometimes quite remote residents of their *desa*. Under these circumstances, mapping village territories can be a dizzying task. In addition, the act of mapping itself sometimes serves as a catalyst for some boundary disputes to be settled and other conflicts to arise. Ambiguity in practice is easy to live with, but disagreement is bound to surface when someone wishes to

(Box continued on next page)

Box 4 (continued)

record boundaries on an official map. Conflict tends to be most common in areas of special economic value, such as good fishing spots, swiftlet caves (for edible birds' nests), and timber in particular. Competing versions of oral history and the promise of financial gain, however slight, at times make these disputes intractable. While ethnicity and village membership certainly matter in the perception of where the boundaries are, village politics and personal affiliations continue to complicate consensus based on ethnic group alone.

Conflicts have intensified with the recent logging boom under decentralization, especially in Kalimantan. Disputes have arisen (or have been rekindled) between neighboring communities when rights either to be compensated for logging or to refuse to log are at issue. Local people recognize that lines are being drawn that will later determine not only who will receive money from logging, but more fundamentally, who has the right to determine the fate of the forest.

These disputes are often damaging to relations between closely related communities. Animosity between communities has crippled some social networks and created a general sense of distrust and disharmony. In one case, a community has delayed building a new longhouse, because unsettled disputes are said to produce supernaturally "hot" conditions, during which ritually sensitive activities must be avoided. Sadly, close kin relations have been attenuated over access to timber and money, the latter of which is not all that much, even in the local context.

In other areas, ambiguity about the edges of village territories is more congenially described as *wilayah kerjasama*, or "cooperation areas." This may be the result of close village ties, such as those that result from close kinship, or the fission of a large village into two. Such cooperative areas may also indicate that as long as the resources involved are not too valuable, ambiguity is permitted. In any case, *kerjasama* areas signify the potential for cooperation among neighboring villages.

Disputes are a natural part of a continual process of renegotiation or reaffirmation between competing parties regarding rights to access and use natural resources. In situations of such complex layering of claims, it is the intensity and forms of dispute management that may be more accurate indicators of unworkable conflict, rather than the mere

(Box continued on next page)

Box 4 (continued)

presence of disagreement. One approach to addressing intractable disputes is to build on indigenous concepts. Joint management rights over a disputed area could be established between the claimants, similar to customary forests shared by multiple forest communities for subsistence use, but protected from commercial extraction.

Community maps will not guarantee enduring clarity or the legal recognition by the state of CBPRs. But there is power in being able to communicate one's own ideas of territory and where the boundaries lie. The increasing grip of international markets and large-scale state-sponsored commercial extraction highlights the importance of defining CBPRs and other local rights in ways that are easily understood by outsiders. Despite the challenges and costs, for resource-dependent local people there may be little other choice.

Sources:

Natalia, Ita. "Protecting and Regaining Dayak Lands through Community Mapping." In *Indigenous Social Movements and Ecological Resilience: Lessons from the Dayak of Indonesia.* Washington, DC: Biodiversity Support Program, 2000.

Harwell, Emily. "The Social Life of Boundaries: Competing Territorial Claims and Conservation Planning in Danau Sentarum Wildlife Reserve, West Kalimantan Indonesia." In *Institutional Context of Biodiversity Maintenance in Asia: Trans-national, Cross-sectoral, and Inter-disciplinary Approaches,* edited by Michael R. Dove. Chicago, IL: MacArthur Foundation. Forthcoming.

Momberg, Frank; Kristianus Atok; and Martua Sirait. *Drawing on Local Knowledge: A Community Mapping Training Manual.* Jakarta, Indonesia: The Ford Foundation, WWF Indonesia Program, and Yayasan Karya Sosial Pancur Kasih, 1996.

Wadley, Reed. R. "Community Co-operatives, Illegal Logging, and Regional Autonomy: Empowerment and Impoverishment in the Borderlands of West Kalimantan, Indonesia." Paper presented at the meeting on Resource Tenure, Forest Management, and Conflict Resolution: Perspectives from Borneo and New Guinea, Australian National University, Canberra, April 9–11, 2001.

number of hectares of concession that overlap with village lands, and the density and cost of each type of tree (meranti, durian, etc.) per hectare. The company agreed to a negotiated amount of Rp 400,000,000 and eventually pulled out of the area altogether. From the settlement, villagers applied Rp 50,000,000 to their village credit union for small loans to community members, and they equitably distributed the rest of the compensation to each household based on how much loss a family had sustained from company activities.

Local community plans in the future include regulating access and use of their own natural resources. For example, the use and access of the swiftlets' caves will not be open to outsiders. Local community members take turns guarding cave entrances to prevent outsiders from entering. In this way, they control the harvest, and outsiders must buy from them.

Recognition of Rattan Gardens Management Systems

The Department of Forestry maintains that rattan is a forest product harvested from the wild and is subject to the harvesting permit system, a system prone to corruption and difficult for local communities to access. If rattan gardens are recognized as agroforestry systems, the permit system should not apply to them. Planted rattan instead would be treated as a regular farm product. *SHK-Kaltim* has undertaken a policy analysis of rattan regulations with the goal of drafting a new local regulation that recognizes rattan gardens as managed agroforestry systems that are exempt from the harvest permit fees and regulations. Environmental economic valuation has also contributed to economic arguments for the recognition of rattan gardens.

Declaration of Protected Area Community-Managed Zones

Lorentz National Park, West Papua

A draft Memorandum of Understanding (MOU) to incorporate community-based management plans into the Lorentz National Park Management Plan is being negotiated between WWF-Sahul and the local planning authority (*Bappeda*). A participatory planning process is underway in two sites: one in Wamena, Ibele, and the other in the Asmat area, Joerat. This planning process will result in community-based management plans or *adat* conservation agreements.

In 1991, local communities of Walesi felt threatened by the plan of the National Power Corporation (PLN) to construct a power plant near Lake Habema. The plant would take control of areas mostly owned by Walesi communities. Elders of the Walesi confederation (*O'o ukul Walesi*) sought advice from the Wamena Archbishop, Franz Lieshouth, on how to best respond. In late 1991, elders of *O'o ukul Walesi* set up a Walesi Adat Deliberation Body, or *Badan Musyawarah Adat Walesi* (BMAW). They assigned a group of Walesi teachers from a church-affiliated primary school in Wamena to become executives of the body. Under the agreement of the elders, some money was collected from the communities (approximately Rp 1,000/ household) to pay for the costs of obtaining legal recognition of this body. BMAW then became the Walesi Adat Development Foundation, or *Yayasan Bina Adat Walesi* (YBAW), with initial capital of Rp 2,500,000 gathered from household contributions.

From 1992 to 1994 YBAW appraised the price of land within the *O'o ukul Walesi* area. YBAW facilitated negotiations between *O'o ukul Walesi* and the PLN until an agreement for compensation was reached. Learning from that success, in early 1995 *O'o ukul* Ibele asked YBAW to assist them in dealing with road construction plans to Lake Habema by the local government of Jayawijaya and the Irian Jaya's Public Works Department. Efforts to address this threat were not as successful as the PLN case, because *O'o ukul* Ibele lost traditional areas without compensation from the local government. Still, elders of *O'o ukul* Ibele agreed to ask YBAW to help them obtain recognition of *adat* CBPRs. In 1996 YBAW collaborated with *O'o ukul* Heatnem and WWF-Lorentz to map the boundaries of Lorentz National Park.

Agreements now reached in Walesi, Heatnem, and Ibele cover

- confederation area boundaries as well as clan-based *adat* areas;
- local land uses;
- protected (sacred) areas;
- limitation on selling land to outsiders; and
- mechanisms for planning and development of public facilities and infrastructure, such as road construction that should involve *adat* institutions.

Adat elders, YBAW, WWF-Sahul, and heads of villages within the Walesi, Heatnem, and Ibele areas actively promote and monitor the agreements related to *adat* rights. In Habema, local communities have expelled outside hunters as well as orchid gatherers in their area. Particularly in Walesi and Ibele, *adat* elders oblige tourists to have local guides. This prevents outside hunters and orchid gatherers from trespassing within traditional areas. The local government, however, has yet to show its disagreement or agreement with these processes and the positive field results.

Learning from the long process of consensus building, YBAW identified six enabling conditions needed to achieve and maintain community-based management authority over *adat* territories:

1. early agreement among *adat* institutions to manage areas collaboratively so that threats and benefits are shared;
2. agreement among *adat* institutions to identify clear boundaries of areas to be managed collaboratively;
3. agreement among *adat* institutions to assign an independent institution to become coordinator and communicator of *adat* area management;
4. knowledge and information about resource potentials within the managed area;
5. agreement among *adat* institutions to establish local use regulations that accommodate both *adat* rules and the official state regulations; and
6. recognition by various parties of the *adat* managed area (the territory), the local use regulations, and the institution.

YBAW and WWF-Sahul monitor the implementation of the agreements using these six enabling conditions. YBAW has found that the local actors respect and recognize the agreements. YBAW now uses the six enabling conditions to help build constituencies, particularly with other large Jayapura-based organizations, such as WWF-Sahul, LPPMA, YPLHC, and Konpenma, as well as local legislative members.

Tangkoko Nature Reserve, North Sulawesi

KEMALA partner, Forum Petaupan Katouan (FPK)-Yayasan Kelola helped local communities in Pinangunian, Makawidey, Batuputih, and Kasawari to conduct participatory rural appraisal (PRA) and community mapping and to develop village information systems. These four traditional villages are adjacent to Tangkoko-Dua Basudara Nature Reserve in Bitung, North Sulawesi. The results of their activities were presented in 1999 to the provincial office of Nature Conservation and Preservation (PKA) in a workshop conducted by community organizers from the villages. The main purpose was to show PKA that local communities could effectively participate in the sustainable management of natural resources within the reserve. The communities learned from the success story of other villagers adjacent to Bunaken National Park. They also informed local nature conservation officers in Tangkoko that the presence of a mining company in the area disturbs their own management processes.

Originally, only organizers from Kasawari and Pinangunian were able to reach an agreement with the Bitung Timur sub-district government. Their success was based upon FPK's organizer from *Kelola* who had helped navigate the process with the district government of Bolang Mangondouw. All four villages have now reached the same agreement with the PKA authority, as well as with the Bitung Timur sub-district government. The Bitung Timur sub-district government committed to issuing a decree recognizing the community maps that show the revised boundaries between the villages and the reserve and to establishing local participation in nature reserve patrols to prevent timber stealing and hunting of wildlife in the reserve. This will help enable other villages to do likewise.

Lore Lindu National Park (Central Sulawesi)—Recognition of Community Control over Adat *Territory within National Park Boundaries*

An important policy initiative was adopted in April 1999 that has already shown significant improvements in central Sulawesi. The Katu tribe received a formal decree issued by the head of the Lore Lindu National Park recognizing their rights to continue to live in and control their *adat* territory. The decree covers an area of 1178 ha within the boundaries of the 220,000 ha national park. The head of the national park said that he was convinced that the Katu land management practices were environmentally sustainable.

With assistance from a number of Central Sulawesi members of JKPP, the Katu produced a survey report on traditional management practices and a series of maps including an *adat* lands reference map, an *adat* agro-forest map, and a natural resources map. The report revealed richly diverse agricultural practices involving thirty-three local rice varieties, eight varieties of sweet potatoes, eight varieties of maize, and six different varieties of yams. Another feature documented by the survey was the pattern of natural resource use employed by the Katu, who have been harvesting wood, rattan, damar, and a number of non-timber forest products in a sustainable way for centuries. This information was used in an ongoing dialogue between the Katu people and the government. It was also used to run a high-profile media campaign that gained significant coverage from the electronic and print media at the regional and national levels.

The Katu have proven to be more effective than the park rangers in keeping illegal loggers and poachers from operating in their part of the national park. Since the tribe's rights to control their *adat* forests have been recognized, no poachers have been able to enter this area. Previously, people who were harvesting rattan and other forest products frequently entered the area illegally. This has now been stopped entirely, while the Katu themselves observe strict rules in harvesting rattan and other forest products, ensuring regeneration by not over-harvesting. Furthermore, only certain areas of their *adat* territory can be harvested. Other areas are designated for conservation and protected by *adat* rules. Following this success, the national park head issued a second decree recognizing the CBPRs of the Robo Behoa people to their *adat* territory of Doda. This area, based on community maps, covers more than 5000 hectares within the boundaries of Lore Lindu National Park.

Meru-Betiri National Park, East Java

Villagers living in and around the Meru-Betiri National Park in East Java, especially in villages around Andongsari, have been accessing portions of the park, harvesting medicinal plants and other products for daily consumption. The government had branded several of these "entries" as violations of park rules, and this caused tension and conflict between villagers and park managers.

Now, four villages are managing traditional-use zones within the Meru-Betiri National Park. Their aim is to protect the park from outside intrusions and illegal occupation. The village rehabilitation groups (see section above) and LATIN were delegated by the District

Head of Jember, East Java and the Director General for Nature
Conservation (PKA) with responsibility for rehabilitation and
management of the buffer zone (now called traditional-use zone) of
the park. The PKA Director General's office signed an agreement
supporting collaborative efforts between Meru-Betiri National Park
authorities and LATIN to work with local communities and Bogor
Agricultural Institute's forestry faculty to rehabilitate the park. Another
document from the PKA Director General's office defined the
community participants as those living within and adjacent to the
buffer zones of the park. The District Head of Jember formally supported
this arrangement.

Box 5. Conservation and the Denial of Moronene Rights

For over forty years, the Moronene people living within the boundaries
of A'Opa Watumohai National Park in Central Sulawesi have struggled
to gain legal recognition of their CBPRs. Although their rights date
back to the Dutch colonial period, the Moronene have been repeatedly
terrorized by military forces and expelled from their homes and
customary territories. Despite these campaigns of terror and harassment
waged by the provincial government, the Moronene have steadfastly
refused to leave.

In the 1950s, armed bands of the Islamic nationalist movement
Darul Islam/Tentara Islam Indonesia (DI/TII) continually relocated villages
"in the interest of security" and in general brought chaos and fear into
the lives of local villagers, which caused many to flee their homes in
search of safety. In 1970, the area containing the fruit gardens tended
for generations by the Moronene village of Laea Hukea was declared
to be Game Park A'Opa Watumohai and was closed to local use in
order to protect wildlife hunted by local elites. The status changed to
National Park in 1983, and the area was expanded to 105,000 ha,
further removing valuable resources from local use and forcing more
villages to be involuntarily relocated outside of park boundaries. Local
people began writing letters, though unsuccessfully, to park authorities

(Box continued on next page)

Box 5 (continued)

and regional officials—including the park director, the sub-directorate of parks (Kep. Balai PPA), the Governor, and even the Vice-President of Indonesia and the National Commission on Human Rights—to ask that their CBPRs be recognized.

Frustrated by the lack of an official response, the Moronene returned home to their ancestral village of Laea Hukaea. They found that their gardens had been destroyed and, most egregiously, their ancestral gravesites desecrated. Shortly thereafter, those who returned were arrested and charged with violating park boundaries and destroying park resources.

Meanwhile, with the apparent consent and protection of park officials and local government, some residents of nearby towns engaged with impunity in illegal logging within park boundaries. Teak trees claimed by the Moronene were reportedly harvested from the park and used for constructing park offices. Ironically, since the evictions, there has been an increase in poaching in the depopulated park¾gangs of poachers using motor vehicles visit the park nightly to hunt deer and to gather bush meat that is reportedly used by local officials to entertain visiting Jakarta dignitaries.

On December 16, 1997, a delegation from the district government and the parks department negotiated an oral agreement with Laea Hukaea residents that would allow them to remain in the park. Just twelve days later on December 28, 1997, without any discussion or explanation, security forces led by district officials and park personnel attacked the village and burned eighty-eight homes in an operation called "Universal Sweep I" (*Operasi Sapu Jagat* I). This was to be but the first of the most recent violent attacks on local communities.

Operation Universal Sweep II ensued the following year. On October 16, 1998, instructions from the local Bupati ordered all communities within the park to immediately cease all activities, to destroy their houses, and to evacuate the park within five days or be arrested and fined to the full extent of the law. Those who refused were again attacked and had their houses burned. Approximately 175 houses were burned and 300 families evicted. On November 22, 2000, military personnel made the attacks, reportedly on the instruction of the provincial

(Box continued on next page)

Box 5 (continued)

governor Laode Kaimuddin. The security team, consisting of local police, members of the notorious Brimob (mobile brigade) police special forces, plus forest police and officials, again evicted local communities, destroying 100 homes with chainsaws.

The villagers have been pressured to move to a transmigration-style resettlement site in a 700 ha area next to an estate run by the timber conglomerate Barito Pacific in the Rarowatu subdistrict. There, each family will only have a 2-ha plot on which to support themselves instead of being able to practice their traditional, extensive form of agro-forestry.

According to WALHI, the provincial government is driving the latest wave of evictions, not the park authorities, who are now reported to acknowledge the Moronene's role in conservation. WALHI asserts that local economic interests are prompting the evictions. The area is included in the Buton-Kolaka-Kendari Integrated Economic Development Zone (Kapet), and suspicions are rife that the Moronene have been moved to give investors access to park resources. With the new emphasis on regional autonomy, some local officials are scrambling to grant commercial industries legal access to natural resources in order to generate income for their administrations and, frequently, themselves.

The Moronene are not unique in having their rights violated, ostensibly to protect natural resources—in areas that, once depopulated, are then logged. During September and October 1990, *Operasi Senyum* (Operation Smile) used military personnel to force 1735 households (6470 people) from their homes in the Pulau Panggung Protected Area in South Lampung and resettled them in a transmigration area of Rawajitu, South Lampung (Fay et al. 1999, 7). In January and February 1995, *Operasi Jagawana* (Operation Forest Ranger) used elephants to destroy 4000 ha of coffee farms and houses and drove 474 households (2400 people) from their homes in Dwikora, Bukit Kemuning and out of the Tangkit Tebak Protected Area in North Lampung (Ibid).

Adapted from:
Adi Jaya, Sarlan. "Legal and Social Justice Issues in Natural Resource Management: The Case of the Moronene People of A'Opa Watumohai National Swampland Park."
Down to Earth 41:6, 48: 2
Kendari Pos 30 Nov. 2000, 12 Jan. 2001;
Suara Pembaruan 1 Dec. 2000.

The four villages managing the park are Andongrejo, Curahnongko, Sanenrejo, and Wonosari, all in the sub-district of Temorejo, District of Jember, East Java. Management responsibilities consist not only of growing specified trees and plants supplied by the park authority to rehabilitate the area, but also ensuring that village sources of livelihoods and staple foods are maintained. The initial conflict between local people and the park authority has almost completely dissipated because of this management agreement. From the 7-ha demonstration plot for herbal medicine gardens in 1993, the area has now expanded to cover approximately 1300 ha where medicinal plants are interspersed with park rehabilitation crops and staple foods. The demonstration plot has grown over, and its canopy is now closed. Birds have returned to the area, and community members continue to harvest their medicinal products from it. This demonstration plot shows what the local communities intend to do with the other areas assigned to them.

Politically, the communities are aware of the need to establish networks. They have an Inter-Village Coordination Forum both at the district and sub-district levels. In Jember, a local organization, the Andongrejo Village Information Center, hosted a discussion where the local legislature and executive presented planned legislation to recognize community participation in natural resource management.

To help establish a community-managed zone in Meru-Betiri National Park, LATIN worked with the local organization, *Kelompok TOGA Sumber Waras* (KTSW), to replant many of the medicinal plant species found in the park. LATIN assisted with finding the necessary capital to start processing raw materials into a medicinal drink mix. Villagers then applied for a license to market these medicines. Nine village health centers are now opting for herbal medicines, supported by a directive of the Department of Health (which resulted from discussing this initiative of the villagers), and are obtaining their supplies of herbal medicines from KTSW.

After presenting the results of this community initiative at the sub-district government health office, KTSW was invited to extend its reach to fifty more health centers in the area during 2001. Local government now supports this group with equipment to process the medicinal plants more efficiently. It also provided training and infrastructure for the village units. They have received visitors and apprentices from local communities in East and West Nusa Tenggara.

With the issuance of the license, villagers have been able to better manage their time. Women maintain the herbal gardens and assist in processing the medicines, while men clear and plant not only medicinal plants and staple foods, but also the trees required for the rehabilitation of the park. They also organize the harvesting of the products.

Conflicts with Extraction: Recognition of Community Management Agreements

Tanggerang, Ketapang District, West Kalimantan

Local communities in the Tanggerang area of West Kalimantan have become aware of threats to their natural resources and livelihoods that are posed by an increasing number of activities. These include palm oil and industrial tree plantations, community logging, natural disasters (e.g., drought leading to forest fires and locust plagues on rice fields), and the destruction of various agroforestry and forest silvicultural systems.

There are no more primary forestlands in the area of Tanggerangn, which is the center for *Me'adati Buah,* a customary practice that ensures that local communities actualize principles of ecological balance in daily activities. Economic crisis led many local community members to cut valuable timber species (also endemic and endangered) including ironwood, *bengkirai,* and *sungkai.* The communities felt that this logging resulted in negative impacts on watersheds, including floods, soil erosion, and pollution of downstream rivers, which are clogged with loose logs. In the communities living downstream, skin diseases occur as wastes and log preservatives accumulate in choke points where logs obstruct stream flow. The oil palm plantation companies PT Golden Hope and PT Poly Plan tried to acquire rights to community *adat* land by offering huge sums of money to targeted individuals willing to sell.

In response to these problems, community mapping and management planning was undertaken with the help of PPSDAK in Tanjung, Pasir Mayang, Sungai Kiriq, Penggerawan, and Pangkalan Pakit. After the traditional village territories had been mapped, members from each local community met to discuss management plans and to develop a joint agreement. It specifically obliges community members "to support the customary and cultural practices for management and conservation of natural resources inside the *adat* area of Tanggerang." Community and government representatives signed the map in May 2000. It is now used, along with their management plans, to keep investors Golden Hope and Poly Plan from entering the Tanggerang village areas.[5]

Balai Semandang, Ketapang District, West Kalimantan

Villagers discovered that the Ketapang district government had issued the oil palm company PT Bakrie Brothers Plantation II a license for a 13,000-hectare concession, without any notification to or consent from the affected community on whose land the plantation was to be located. The company conducted field surveys but did not consult with the local community before setting up the boundary markers.

The villagers discovered the surveyors and took them to their *adat* leaders. A dialogue ensued between the community and the company, during which the villagers showed the company their community maps. Villagers explained that they could not agree to convert farmlands and orchards (*tembawangs*) into timber plantations, because the land is their life and culture and is also part of the last remaining forests in the world.[6] Eventually, the company withdrew. The community then set up their own markers in the boundaries of their territory.

Resak Balai[7] and Tapang Sambas-Tapang Kemayau,[8] Sanggau District, West Kalimantan

Local communities were concerned with increasing logging in Resak Balai and the oil palm plantation of PT Multi Prima Entakai in Tapang Sambas-Tapang Kemayau. They decided to reassess their local *adat* law to make it relevant to current problems of logging and plantation intrusion, and specifically to address the problems of dwindling forest resources and the need for tougher sanctions. They conducted mapping and jointly signed agreements.

Advances in traditional village, NGO, and local government relations in Sanggau have resulted in the formal recognition of CBPRs and management authority. Local communities have also been successful in negotiating government approval in the form of local legislation recognizing these initiatives (or *Perda, peraturan daerah*). DPRD Sanggau has listed as priority legislation those related to village land use, village governance, and village forests. Pancur Kasih NGOs received direct requests for assistance from the local legislature in Sanggau in drafting these priority regulations.

Empetai⁹ Sanggau District, West Kalimantan

The Sanggau district has been declared as a Designated Integrated Economic Development Zone (KAPET), which has rapidly increased the expansion of oil palm concessions. In response to threats that local communities perceived to their natural resources, like the case above, the Merbang people agreed to map their territory and to strengthen their management practices and sanctions within that territory. These community agreements have been submitted to the Sanggau legislature as evidence of the communities' management plans and rights. These maps and regulations were presented to the Sanggau DPRD. Improved opportunities to negotiate recognition of this form of village governance and management come with the overall Pancur Kasih NGOs strategy to work with the Sanggau DPRD.

Kotup, West Kalimantan

Local communities became concerned about the activities of small-scale gold miners using suction machines on the land (locally called *Dompeng*) and about their support from outside business interests. These concerns were the catalyst for formalizing community regulations and sanctions to get government support and recognition. After confiscating the excavation equipment and expelling the businessman leasing them, community maps were made in three main villages, Kotup, Tebilai, Tembawang, and a joint agreement, facilitated by the Pancur Kasih consortium, was reached. This agreement included prohibitions of forest burning, commercial logging, and fish poisoning.

Bukit Sapatutn River Basin Agreement, Menjalin, West Kalimantan

Downstream from a key river basin that feeds into the Kapuas River, a small community mapped its area and found its rivers badly damaged from activities of villagers upstream. Fish catches were low, diseases attributed to the polluted and poisoned river water increased, and drought brought additional aggravations. Upon the recommendation of villagers downstream, using *adat binua* structures, nine villages composed of areas upstream and downstream of the river basin of *Nyawan* and *Mempawah* rivers in Pontianak Regency, in a special *adat* ceremony, signed an agreement and resolved to

- protect the tributaries and the rivers around the *Nyawan* and *Mempawah* rivers;
- prohibit fishing using chemical poisons;
- prohibit cutting of timber in protected forests that are watersheds;
- protect all sacred areas in each of the nine villages; and
- fine all violations using *adat* law (6 *tahil tangah jubata*, 3 *buah siam yaitu siam pahar, siam batu dan siam jarikng*).

One year after the agreement was formalized, no poison was used in large rivers, only in smaller tributaries, and poison used for fishing was only from local tree species (*Derris sp.*). A drastic reduction in timber cutting in *adat* protected and sacred areas was also noted. Hardwood trees were being increasingly planted in the villages (based on monitoring in two among nine villages).

Decentralization has also created new opportunities, because this area falls under the new sub-district of Bengkayang. A DPRD training session in the area led to collaborative plans with Pancur Kasih NGOs to work with local government and the DPRD to develop village management and governance regulations.

Co-Management Agreement at Nain, North Sulawesi

The Nain island communities have experienced rapid economic change since the expansion of seaweed cultivation on the coast. Most residents have shifted their primary livelihoods from fishing to planting seaweeds. The destruction of mangroves and upland forests on the coast, not only on Nain Island but also on other neighboring islands, has ensued. KEMALA partner FPK facilitated village meetings to discuss the implications of this environmental degradation, including the depletion of local wells. The inequity of an economic benefit for some that resulted in loss to others was seen as a crucial problem that needs to be addressed.

At a village meeting the residents formulated an agreement to (1) stop cutting and attempt to replant the mangrove, (2) stop cutting upland trees and replant using fruit trees, and (3) limit seaweed cultivation to certain zones. The community will collaborate with the village government in the monitoring of the implementation of agreement.

Building for the Future

As the foregoing information from the field demonstrates, there is unprecedented change underway in rural communities throughout Indonesia. The inertia of the new administration and reform cabinet, rather than instilling hardened cynicism or reckless optimism, should serve as a warning that crucial reforms still must be made. During this time of opportunity, it is vital that local community concerns are meaningfully and wisely addressed and that the unjust and destructive policies of collusion between resource extraction industries and government are no longer aided and abetted. The recognition of community-based *adat* property rights and the promulgation and institutionalizing of fair resource management policies are key. They have enormous potential to contribute to the reconciliation and stability of the world's fourth most populous nation, home to some of the planet's richest and rarest ecosystems and to the millions of people who manage and depend on them.

Notes

1. Pemberdayaan Pengelolaan Sumber Daya Alam Kerakyatan (PPSDAK)- Pancur Kasih.

2. Yayasan Bina Adat Walesi (YBAW), WWF-Sahul, LATIN (*Lembaga Alam Tropika Indonesia*) and JKPP (Jaringan Kerja Pemetaan Partisipatif)

3. Pemberdayaan Pengelolaan Sumber Daya Alam Kerakyatan (PPSDAK)- Pancur Kasih.

4. Timber harvest was formerly regulated by village adat rules: e.g., no one is allowed to cut trees with a diameter less than seven hands, fingers stretched out (~30 centimeters diameter at breast height (dbh)), and only in areas zoned by the community for commercial harvest. Recently, the increase in price for sawn logs has increased cutting. In contrast, rubber used to yield relatively high prices. In Sungai Utik (Kab. Kapuas Hulu) alone, 32 households harvest approximately 1,500 kg of rubber a day. In

one month (20 days of work) 30,000 kg can be harvested, which sells for Rp 1,800 per kg (Rp 54,000,000 income for the village) and provides at least Rp 1,700,000 per family.

5. For additional information see: Dove, M. R. "Plantation Development in West Kalimantan II: The Perceptions of the Indigenous Population." *Borneo Research Bulletin* 18, no. 1 (1986), 3–27.

6. See documentation entitled: *"Bagaimana Mempertahankan Tanah Adat? Belajar dari Pengalaman Masyarakat Balai Semandang,"* by Pancur Kasih, 1998.

7. See documentation entitled: *"Hukum Adat Tentang Pengelolaan Lingkungan Adat: Adat Ngau Ngatur Tanah Ai', Babas-Rima', Gupung-Julut, Buah-Layah",* 10 May 1996, PPSDAK File.

8. See documentation entitled: *"Pekat Adat Masyarakat Tapang Sambas-Tapang Kemayau: Hukum Adat Tentang Pengelolaan Lingkungan Adat"* 15 January 1998, PPSDAK File.

9. See documentation entitled: "Kesepakatan Adat Pengelolaan Sumber Daya Alam Oleh Masyarakat Adat," 9 August 1999, PPSDAK File.

V.

NEW STATES...NEW ASSUMPTIONS?

The year 1997 heralded dramatic change for Indonesia. In the autumn of that year, the value of the national currency fell in just a few months from 2400 rupiah (Rp) to the U.S. dollar to a low of 17,000 Rp. Inflation soared to 80%, and the economy contracted by 14%. Over 8 million people lost their jobs. Real wages declined by 35% in 1998, while food prices increased by 115% (World Bank 1998). At the same time, drought ruined harvests, and widespread forest fires consumed more than 7 million hectares,[1] largely due to illegal land clearing at the behest of plantation concessionaires. This trans-boundary disaster brought sharp criticism from international observers and even from the historically noninterventionist governments of the Association of South East Asian Nations (ASEAN).[2] Increasing unrest and demonstrations throughout Indonesia, much of it fueled by local conditions described in this report, culminated with violent student and military clashes in Jakarta. Widespread rioting ensued, and New Order President Suharto's 32-year long rule abruptly ended on May 21, 1998.

Following the resignation of Suharto, long-smoldering separatist movements in East Timor, West Papua,[3] and Aceh[4] increased in intensity, as did violent military suppression of them.[5] In addition to a desire for cultural and political autonomy, these and most other provinces aspire for more fairness in the allocation of legal and economic benefits from natural resources. The presence of oil and gas in Timor and Aceh and of gold, other minerals, and timber in West Papua greatly influences both the desire for independence in these regions and the strength of Indonesian nationalist opposition to it.

While these provinces have long histories of independence movements—East Timor has since successfully gained political independence[6]—many other provinces saw presidential succession as an opportunity to press for more political power and a more equitable share of the economic benefits derived from the exploitation of natural resources within their own territories. Local governments and people throughout the vast archipelagic nation voiced frustration at the economic and political injustices of the last thirty-two years by asserting their rights and in some instances by reclaiming land expropriated from them for plantations, golf courses, and timber concessions.[7] Discontent and violence boiled over in many regions of the country, and in many instances those who saw political benefits fanned the flames. The transition government under B. J. Habibie quickly turned to decentralization as an antidote to the growing threat of disintegration and to establish itself as a legitimate reform government.

In the summer of 1999, Indonesia held its first free election in forty years. A fledgling democracy began to emerge, and in this new era of reform, unprecedented space opened for debate that includes alternative viewpoints. This energized a multilateral push for change on fundamental questions about state laws and policies, including those pertaining to the legal recognition of *adat* CBPRs and local community participation in natural resource management. Restrictions on political parties were lifted, and the number of political parties increased from three to forty-eight. Civil society likewise began to develop exponentially. The press, citizen and NGO activists, and even government officials themselves are now freer to voice opposition to state policies than ever before.

NGOs in particular have developed a strong voice in public debates on national laws and policies. Some have even advised the government on policy reform and institutional restructuring, even drafting progressive new legislation.[8] It remains unclear how seriously the new input from civil society will be considered, especially ideas that threaten the state-centric status quo. The legislative process still lacks transparency, as the experience with the new forestry legislation discussed below demonstrates. Although there is heated (and healthy) debate about the true depth of commitment to legislative and regulatory reform, there has been greatly increased involvement by various constituencies in law and policy-making processes, including those that resulted in constitutional amendments in 2000.[9]

As October 2002 commenced, the Constitution had been amended to include human rights protections (Article 28, Sections E-J), including recognition of community-based *adat* rights. Article 28 H now provides for the "right of every citizen to prosperity, a place of residence, and a safe and clean environment." Article 28 I "guarantees that cultural identity and traditional rights be respected in accordance with their development over time." Finally, Article 18 B specifically provides for the "recognition and respect of the unity of traditional communities and their traditional rights as long as they continue to exist and are in accordance with the principle of the United Nation of Indonesia, which is ordered by law." All of these progressive developments reflect the rapidly changing policy environment in Jakarta. They provide for some optimism about prospects for meaningful reforms that address the needs and aspirations of rural Indonesians who are directly dependent on natural resources. As highlighted throughout this report, now is the time for creative thinking on new legal arrangements that can help to stem the tide of unsustainable natural resource degradation and help to promote environmental justice and local well-being.

There is also reason for caution, as much of the legal and policy infrastructure of the dictatorship remains unchanged. Although Suharto is no longer physically present in the Presidential Palace, he, his family, and other New Order adherents still have a large presence in Indonesia as they elude prosecution for their embezzlement and other forms of corruption that impoverished the nation and hastened its environmental degradation.[10] Incredibly, even Suharto's closest associates (among them Harmoko, the head of the corrupt former ruling party GOLKAR say "down with corruption, collusion and nepotism."[11] They do this while many beneficiaries of the New Order administration remain in place at central, regional, and local level administrations and the institutional culture of state privilege remains largely intact in the minds of many officials. Despite Suharto's fall, the parliamentary assemblies (MPR and DPR) that were themselves the products of fraudulent elections remained in place to oversee the subsequent elections and "reform" administrations.

Even at the highest levels, political struggles over who will be the heirs of the post–New Order regime continue. Abdurahman Wahid ascended to the Presidency in late 1999 amid a splintered opposition by making strategic alliances with GOLKAR and the military and by breaking with his old ally Megawati and her Indonesian Democratic Party (PDI).[12] Critically, Wahid incurred political debts that crippled his ability to make a true break with the neo-colonial past. This ultimately ensured a failure to move forward on anticipated reforms.[13] As the economy continued to stagnate and human rights reforms continued to languish, discontent mounted on all sides. The parliament eventually voted to impeach the beleaguered Wahid. In a final effort to stay in power, Wahid attempted to dissolve the parliament, but the military refused to act on his commands. On July 23, 2001, Vice-President Megawati Sukarnoputri, daughter of the first President Sukarno, was sworn in as the new president of Indonesia, surrounded by congratulatory military brass.

The political influence of crony capitalism may now be more covert than in the past, when timber barons golfed and fished with Suharto. But the protracted search for Suharto's son Tommy (who was convicted on corruption charges and implicated in the murder of the judge who presided over his trial), illustrates that decades of nepotistic relations will not be easily cast aside, either at the highest levels of central government or at the desks of more lowly government officials, where most local people encounter the state.

In addition, one of the quickest ways for Indonesia to generate capital to pay back its International Monetary Fund (IMF) "rescue" loan is through the forestry and plantation sectors, which the IMF has specifically supported through programs that encourage foreign investment. As a result, logging booms (by enterprises on both international and village-level scales) and the expansion of oil-palm plantations have exploded. Many areas have already become "Designated Integrated Economic Development Zones" (KAPET, or *Kawasan Pembangunan Ekonomi Terpadu*) specifically targeted for plantation development, largely for oil palm.

In a report released in October 2001 by the World Wildlife Fund and the Indonesia-based Center for International Forestry Research (CIFOR), the World Bank and IMF are blamed for encouraging speculative investment in the forest sector and increased timber harvesting by debt-ridden Indonesian pulp and paper companies.

The report argues that forestry reforms mandated by a US$43 billion IMF emergency financial package in 1999 are based in large part on faulty assumptions and have promoted increased rates of timber harvesting. It also asserts that the IMF mandated reforms largely overlook the expansion of Indonesia's timber plantations and pulp and paper industries (Barr 2001; Mainhardt 2001).[14]

These trends suggest that the development imperatives pursued under the New Order and World Bank/IMF have endured largely unchanged during the initial post-Suharto era. This does not bode well for Indonesia's struggling democracy, its shrinking and rapidly degrading natural resource base, or for its impoverished and marginalized majority.

Decentralization and Community Rights in the Post-Suharto Era

Decentralization of government and fiscal control in Indonesia was first mandated by the parliament under transition-President Habibie[15] and was later hastily written into law as Law No. 22/1999 on Regional Autonomy and Law No. 25/2000 on Fiscal Decentralization. In theory, these laws allow provinces to be essentially self-governing except for a few key areas (foreign policy, national security, judiciary, fiscal policy, and religion). Notably, they also empower provinces to issue use permits[16] and directly access economic benefits from natural resource enterprises. One decentralization consultant remarked privately that these new laws represent some of the most ambitious decentralization initiatives attempted anywhere in the world. Many doubts remain as to how and whether they will be implemented.[17] In fact, as this report goes to press, actions are underway to reassert the preeminent role of the central government with greater oversight and control of district level legislation.[18]

One key change in the decentralization reform that merits continuation is the repeal of Law No. 5/1979 on Village Administration. The repealed law imposed uniform and unaccountable administrative structures that undermined the autonomy of traditional village institutions and governance, a topic explored in detail in Chapter II. Under the new decentralization law, village governance may now take diverse and locally appropriate forms, and leadership is no longer to be controlled by the central government. This is a remarkable milestone in restoring democratic control over village affairs to local communities. Yet the form that the new village government is to take will be determined by regional regulations (*perda*), which are still largely unwritten. How innovative these regulations will be, and who will actually get to participate in their crafting, remains to be seen. The extent of control that the new heirs of regional autonomy—the *Bupatis* and *Camats* (district and sub-district heads)—will have over village leadership and decision-making also remains an open question (Casson 2001; Rhee 2000).[19] Likewise, the overall impact of undercutting the authority of provincial government (which in many cases has been the locus of political discontent towards the central administration) in favor of district officials is also a concern.

As noted in Chapter I, decentralization and devolution of government authority are fundamentally different from community-based natural resource management (CBNRM), and the need in many cases is for legal recognition of CBPRs. CBNRM is still all too often considered to be a variant of decentralization, and this is a serious error. The

---

Box 6. Community Co-operatives, Illegal Logging, and Regional Autonomy: Empowerment and Impoverishment in the Borderlands of West Kalimantan

Illegal logging has increased dramatically across the country since the onset of the Indonesian economic crisis in 1997. In West Kalimantan, Indonesia, these activities have invariably involved the export of timber across the porous international border into Sarawak, Malaysia (the same holds true for East Kalimantan, with timber going into Sabah, Malaysia).

The power vacuum left after the end of Suharto's New Order regime has resulted in a *de facto* regional autonomy, well prior to the implementation of formal decentralization in 2001, which continues to facilitate these logging and export activities.

In the borderland of the upper Kapuas, West Kalimantan, local elites and Malaysian timber bosses have taken advantage of the situation and of a new forestry law permitting community cooperatives to cut timber for sale, creating a mini-economic boom.

(Box continued on next page)

Box 6 (continued)

Today in the upper Kapuas borderland, local communities and Malaysian financiers are the chief players, rather than the Indonesian concessionaires. In February 2000, there were at least twelve small financiers (*tauke*) from Sarawak operating in border locations along a stretch of about 40 km. Their numbers may continue to grow. Six of these *tauke* have built substantial sawmills near the main government road that runs just south of the border. It is almost certain that the area being logged will be expanded to accommodate these sawmills.

Much of the logging being carried out in 2000 was through community co-operatives organized by savvy liaisons, both residents or non-residents, with ties to the timber industry and to local, regional, and provincial government; and company bosses in Malaysia. For a fee (US$10 to $60), these handlers negotiate with timber company representatives and their contractors. Some of these liaisons control co-op members' access to information (and bargaining positions) and to the timber company representatives. Some also receive salaries from the timber companies.

Co-ops receive modest commissions for the wood cut in their forests (US$2.52 to $4.46 per cubic meter). Once taken across the border to Malaysia, however, the timber is milled and exported to Japan, Taiwan and Hong Kong at an export price of US$340 per cubic meter, on average. This means that co-ops receive commissions generally amounting to *less than 1% of the export value of the wood*. But these commissions are much more than communities ever received from logging companies in the past.

Locals are still bitter over their lack of profit from past logging operations.

All co-ops appear to have proper permits issued through the regional office for development cooperatives. But few permits conform to existing regulations for legal timber cutting or for establishing sawmills. Further, there is no indication that profits from the logging are divided out among the member communities; instead, each community appears to be acting independently and receiving commissions on logging by itself.

Additionally, in at least one case of heated disputes between communities over forest land, the disputing communities belonged to the same co-op. This all suggests that timber companies are using the co-operative permitting system and the prevailing rhetoric about

(Box continues on next page)

Box 6 (continued)

community co-ops to gain access to forest that is now in the hands of communities.

In the past, communities that fell within the concessions had little power over their forests. Now even Indonesian timber companies with concessions elsewhere in the province are hiring community negotiators and public relations officers to handle local community demands for more compensation. Both foreign and domestic timber companies must cooperate more publicly with local communities, and co-ops are how they are doing this. Locals see co-ops as ways to derive some benefit from the forests that have in the past, and might again, become alienated from their control.

The co-op system, however, is just as steeped in corruption as the previous concessions. *Tauke* and their liaisons are said to pay off local police, military, *camat*, and even officials in the *bupati*'s office on a regular basis. In exchange, these civil servants ignore the logging and daily export of wood across the border. Some local residents unconnected to logging are increasingly bitter over this corruption, once again seeing the wealth of their forests and, in some cases, the land itself going to outsiders despite increased community involvement in the process.

Local residents and businessmen are looking forward to formal regional autonomy, but they say the cost for doing business will increase, with even greater corruption. And the potential for severe environmental degradation appears to be a consistent worry resulting from formal autonomy, not to mention conflict over its implementation and even its very meaning. Logging will continue at its current accelerated pace, with operations expanding into areas farther from the border, and particularly along the main government road. Once most of the marketable timber has been cut (and most agree that there is currently enough for five years), conversion to oil palm plantations will likely follow.

Adapted from:
Wadley, Reed. R. "Community Co-operatives, Illegal Logging, and Regional Autonomy: Empowerment and Impoverishment in the Borderlands of West Kalimantan, Indonesia." Paper presented at the meeting on Resource Tenure, Forest Management, and Conflict Resolution: Perspectives from Borneo and New Guinea, Australian National University, Canberra, April 9–11, 2001.

mistake is rooted in a state-centric conceptualization, which assumes that all power and legal rights to natural resources emanate from the nation-state where the natural resources are situated.

Decentralization involves transferring power and authority downward within governmental frameworks. Decentralization, of course, may be complementary to and supportive of CBNRM and the legal recognition of CBPRs. But it is fundamentally different unless local communities are recognized as the first local government unit. True decentralization, not commonly seen, makes a direct connection to CBPRs and involves the state transfer of authority to the locally formed communities.

Decentralization offers potentially important opportunities for local communities to participate in natural resource planning and management and to enjoy more equitable access to economic benefits from the natural resources in their home territories. These goals, however, still remain largely rhetorical. How much authority Indonesia's central government will relinquish, especially related to valuable resources such as timber and minerals, and how much of a role local communities will effectively be allowed to play, are still unclear. Decentralization is devolution of administrative power to local governments and is in itself no guarantee of local community rights or benefits. The questions of *what* is being devolved *to whom* remain unanswered. Will the new "local" leaders be more accountable and representative than those in Jakarta? Is one large, remote feudal state being traded in for many smaller feudal states closer to home?[20] These are questions in need of urgent attention in the months and years ahead.

The struggle for more democratic benefit-sharing and more diffuse local control over natural resources, meanwhile, has also contributed to four interrelated developments: increasing conflict and violence, decentralization of government, the promulgation of a Revised Forestry Law, and increased attention to "people's economy," including moves toward the legal recognition of indigenous peoples' (*masyarakat adat*) rights. All of these developments have important implications for Indonesia and the role of local communities in natural resource management. There is now an unprecedented and urgent opportunity to define the outcomes of these developments to ensure that they contribute to more equitable and sustainable resource management in Indonesia. It is a time of great possibilities and great challenges, with decentralization and community-based management being of foremost importance to many reformists.

The Forestry Bureaucracy

The extent to which power will be devolved under regional autonomy depends largely on what is at stake. Forestry is one of the most lucrative sectors in resource-rich Indonesia, contributing 20% of the national foreign exchange, with revenues in 1998 totaling US$8.5 billion (second only to oil; World Bank 2000b).[21] As has already been noted, it is also one of the most poorly managed from an environmental perspective. The overall deforestation rate in the Outer Islands has been 1.7 million ha per year during the past decade (World Bank 2000a). Significantly, the World Bank now notes that in Indonesia "the smallholder category has been overrated as a cause of deforestation.... The overall impact of swidden farming on forest cover is relatively small" (World Bank 2001, 13; see also Sunderlin and Resosudarmo 1996).

The small operations of illegal loggers, who are funded and protected by local elites and officials, have been identified as key to deforestation. Agus Purnomo, executive director of WWF-Indonesia, estimates that 40 percent of log inputs to these pulp and paper mills are from domestic sources and that 75 percent of this timber has been illegally cut. According to Purnomo, "The scale of illegal logging is huge," and is estimated to be between $4 billion and $6 billion per year.[22]

Under decentralization, both illegal and quasi-legal (because corrupt village leaders make secret deals with the loggers to allow timber harvests without local community consent) logging has vastly accelerated. Forestry officials themselves have openly admitted that illegal logging exceeds legal logging (estimated at 56.6 million ha annually, 70% of total domestic consumption. See Scotland et al. 1999), thereby making the annual cut two to three times larger than what the Ministry considers sustainable (World Bank 2001).

Since the fall of Suharto, mining and forestry/estate crops have been the focus of much regional discontent and much legislative reform. These lucrative sectors have also been given priority attention by the World Bank and IMF and, unsurprisingly, have been the most resistant to decentralization. Some progress has been made. This includes the first devolution of forest management under "special use" community permits, the expansion of commercial use permits to include community institutions, and the recognition of customary forests as a legal forest category (as discussed below).[23]

Nonetheless, these seminal changes supportive of democratization of access to natural resources have not been decisive. As internal and external reformers battle the entrenched institutional cultures, they encounter a fierce defense of state-centric legal jurisdiction over the management and allocation of valuable resources.[24] Inconsistent policies and retreats on initiatives to promote local participation[25] raise doubts about official commitment to decentralization on national levels.[26] They also reflect a longstanding and persistent distrust of local community capacities.

New legislation as of October 2001, including the new Forestry Law, does not reflect a substantial change in the enduring state-centric management paradigm. The Ministry of Forestry and Estate Crops (MoFEC) remains unwilling or incapable of enforcing regulations aimed at preventing unsustainable commercial logging and land clearing practices. Continued use of inappropriate forest classifications[27] and enduring state assertions of exclusive management authority over community forests continue to inhibit local participation in forest management and to undermine sustainable local practices. Much still seems to depend on the individual personalities of officials and on the occurrence of unique political moments in which change can be made.

Even the basic structure and jurisdiction of MoFEC has been under a waxing and waning tide of consolidation and separation, and has been subjected to varying emphases under different Ministers with diverse experience and interests. After the fall of Suharto, the 1998 "reform cabinet" of transition President B. J. Habibie combined the lucrative Estate Crop (tree plantations) sector previously under the jurisdiction of Agriculture into the Ministry of Forestry (MenHutBun). This consolidation allowed for better coordination of forest policy, as two ministries no longer fought for jurisdiction of forestlands. But centralized legal control over forest resources also made it easier to grant permits for logging concessions and to re-classify forest areas for conversion to plantations, areas deemed to be "no longer productive" for timber. In the 2000 cabinet of President Wahid, both the Ministry of Agriculture (which historically has had a more populist orientation, at least nominally) and the commercially oriented MoFEC were briefly consolidated into one Ministry (*MenTanHut*). It had a much more populist focus and an interest in delineation of *adat* areas. This arrangement lasted only a few months before it was retracted.

What should the organizational structure of the forestry be, and what should its jurisdiction include? How can coordination of multiple sectors be balanced with accountability and the devolution of responsibility? Should the primary institutional goal be the administration of large-scale enterprise or facilitation of small-scale community management? Can it do both? These fundamental but unresolved questions are crucial to the meaningful resolution of conflicts and the promotion of environmental justice throughout Indonesia.

State Forests or Community Forests?[28]

Under the Suharto regime, over 75% of Indonesia's land area was classified as State Forest and placed under the sole jurisdiction of the Ministry of Forestry (World Bank 2000b), including nearly 90% of the Outer Islands. Of this state-controlled forest area (143 million ha), almost half is designated as production forest (64 million ha), which until recently was controlled by only a few dozen business conglomerates and top generals.[29]

This narrow bureaucratic legal authority to control vast areas of land and valuable resources has had four main effects:

- encouraged unsustainable use and has been plagued by poor enforcement of regulations and by a focus on unsustainable extraction (mainly of timber) rather than long-term forest management;
- prioritized business interests over local community interests, and inequitably distributed access to economic benefits from forest resources;
- disregarded and undermined traditional community-based institutions and property rights; and
- ignored community capacities and initiatives for sustainable natural resource management and monitoring.

Box 7. Loir Botor Dingit

Chief Dingit has led the struggle to protect indigenous forests in Indonesia against powerful logging and plantation interests. He is a member of the Bentian, a Dayak tribe that uses a traditional system of rattan cultivation that conserves biodiversity and acts as an important source of income.

In 1993 PT Kalhold Utama, an Indonesian logging company owned by Bob Hasan, bulldozed a number of Bentian rattan forest gardens and gravesites. No investigation of the company was conducted. Instead, Indonesian security forces interrogated Chief Dingit and his supporters. When intimidation did not silence Chief Dingit, the government issued charges of forgery against him. The charges were based on a list that the Chief helped villagers compile detailing the destruction of 2,000 trees and 10,000 rattan plants.

Chief Dingit endured these unsubstantiated accusations for years. Finally, in February 1998, he was unexpectedly summoned to a trial based on the forgery charge. In October 1998, the District Court cleared Chief Dingit of all charges, ordered the government to reimburse his legal costs, and issued precedent-setting statements recognizing the existence of indigenous peoples in Indonesia and their right to protect their territories. Dr. Stephanie Fried of Environmental Defense stated, "The court's landmark decision to recognize the existence of indigenous peoples in Indonesia and their right to protect their forested territories calls into question the right of the Indonesian government to grant large plantation, mining, and logging companies access to forested and other occupied lands, owned, and managed by indigenous people throughout Indonesia."

Chief Dingit received the Goldman Environmental Award in 1997 in recognition of his fight for indigenous rights against powerful business interests, and for his support of the Bentian people's sustainable system of forest management.

Adapted from:
Goldman Environmental Prize, http://www.goldmanprize.org

These longstanding inequities perpetuate environmental injustice throughout Indonesia and have generated widespread support for more fair-minded approaches to natural resource management.

Harbingers of Substantive Reform?

A first, albeit modest, step towards democratic reform by the Ministry of Forestry happened even before the resignation of Suharto. Local *damar*[30] resin farmers from Krui in South Sumatra petitioned for recognition of community rights to their orchards to protect them from being felled for timber or oil palm plantations. NGO mediation by a consortium of local people and NGOs, including ICRAF (International Center for Research on Agroforestry), persuaded then Minister of Forestry Djamaludin to pass what was at the time an unprecedented Ministerial Decree.[31] The decree allowed for the recognition of community usufruct rights to the damar gardens for as long as the mixed gardens remained under managed forest cover and did not expand in size. It was the first-ever devolution of management authority by the forest ministry to an indigenous, community-based institution.[32]

Nevertheless, the decree only authorized the grant of *use* rights. It did not provide for recognition of community-based *adat ownership* rights. Rather the decree provided only for the limited grant on the grounds that anything more would be unconstitutional, a legal interpretation based on Article 33 of the Indonesian constitution (which is discussed in Chapters II and VI).[33] Although the Krui decree set a remarkable precedent, the special status did not satisfy local community demands for full return of their customary lands. Further, the decree has not yet been successfully established in Krui or on other community forestlands overlapping with the business interests of powerful business and political people.[34]

Another effort to correct the skewed legal access to forest resources involves the expansion of the community forestry program within state forest areas. Thirty-five-year[35] renewable permits for both non-timber and timber forest enterprise in production forest, and non-timber in protected forest are now open to local community organizations.[36] There has also been an expressed commitment in the government's Five Year Plan (*Propenas*) and National Legal guidelines (GBHN) to democratic reforms in forestry, including community empowerment and participation.[37] But in general, these initiatives laws only provide for grants of usufruct rights, rather than for any legal recognition of *adat* CBPRs or for management authority in the larger sense (i.e., for cultural or ecosystem values other than timber). To the disappointment of many NGOs who worked on drafting the new regulation, the final version provided no security of tenure as the rights may be revoked by the state at any time (although it does allow for community stewardship contracts). Nor did it resolve overlapping community and concessionaire claims to land and resources.[38] The focus has been on improving "people's economy" rather than legally recognizing CBPRs[39]—implying that broadened participation in commerce is the answer, not a more holistic approach to forest management beyond timber, which would empower local communities to pursue their own management goals (Campbell 2001).

There has been increasing emphasis on the redistribution of economic benefits from forest enterprises,[40] rather than providing for the legal recognition of *adat* CBPRs. The most lucrative forest rights (those for commercial use) are to be granted only to village cooperatives, and not to pre-existing *adat* institutions. The co-op requirement precludes community choice over the nature of management institutions. It artificially isolates local institutions for commercial forest use from customary institutions for other kinds of management and village governance (Wollenberg and Kartodihardjo 2001). It also requires the acquisition of specialized knowledge needed to navigate bureaucratic processes in order to establish a cooperative. Even more troubling, the co-op requirement betrays an underlying distrust of indigenous management institutions. It fails to reflect respect for the diversity of traditional local institutions that is mandated by Article 18 of the Constitution (see Chapter VI).

Severance of commercial pursuits from *adat* institutions will likely compromise the effective functioning of many co-ops as long-term management institutions. The orientation of cooperatives is strictly commercial extraction, not sustainable management. Their bureaucratic and time-limited nature destroys the meaning and therefore the likely effectiveness of co-ops as sustainable local management institutions. And opportunities for abuse are created, because anyone, including timber companies, can form local cooperatives with no provision for accountability to local communities as a whole.[41] Even on a local scale, unaccountable commercial enterprise will not rectify and will likely continue the injustice done by undemocratic resource management.

Revised Basic Forestry Law

The revised Basic Forestry Law No. 41 of 1999 takes several seminal steps towards allowing some local community access to forest resources. The most notable change is that the law establishes a legal category of Customary Forest (*hutan adat*) for management by traditional communities with CBPRs over those resources.[42] Further, access to commercial forest use permits is now legally available to community-based institutions (albeit only through the formation of cooperatives). The new forestry law also makes numerous references to the need to manage forests in more sustainable and equitable ways to promote prosperity. The law also includes specific provisions for local community participation (Wollenberg and Kartodihardjo 2001; Rahardjo 1999). For example,

- Forest planning and classification must give due attention to the rights of the people and ensure the involvement of local forest dependent communities. This includes taking into account the relationship between a local community and the forest, including indigenous knowledge, cultural values, and community aspirations and perceptions (Articles 17 and 23).
- Local communities have the right to information about forest management and planning, and to participate in monitoring (Articles 68 and 69).
- A Forestry Watch Forum (*Forum Pemerhati Kehutanan*) made up of NGOs operating in the forestry sector, community leaders, and professional forestry organizations will serve to increase community participation in the forest industry and to help "formulate and manage [*merumuskan dan mengelola*] community perceptions, aspirations and innovations" as input for the government with respect to policy-making (Article 70, Official Explanation).
- Communities are entitled to file claims in court for damages caused by forest loss (Article 71).

- The state is responsible for addressing community needs in the event of pollution or deforestation that adversely affects community lives (Article 72).

These provisions are progressive and provide hope for meaningful democratic reforms on the ground. Important basic premises in the new forestry law, however, are unchanged from old forestry laws. Legislative revisions typically begin with some justification as to why old laws are no longer suitable. The new forestry law opens without any such justification. More important, it makes no real change in the conventional paradigm. This would require some acknowledgment that the state's long-standing assertions of exclusive legal control over most forest areas is unjust and will end (Tim Kajian Tiga Lembaga 2000). Instead, the Revised Forest Law of 1999 is premised on state retention of the (neo) colonial right of exclusive legal control over forests, including customary *adat* areas. This is revealed in three basic ways:

- **Customary Forests are still classified as State Forest.** This classification is justified by the principle of ultimate state authority over resources and citizens,[43] consistent with the now-familiar New Order interpretation of the Constitution (Article 33), especially as found in previous forestry law. (See Chapter II; for an alternative approach see Chapter VI.)
- *Adat* **CBPRs to Customary Forests are not secure.** The new law reasserts the state's monopoly power both to recognize (based on state-determined criteria set out in regional government regulations) and to rescind legal recognition of Customary Forest and of Customary Communities themselves.[44] Ample loopholes authorize the state unilaterally to reclaim valuable forest resources on the grounds that an *adat* community is "no longer in existence." Provisions for recognizing local CBPRs to *hutan adat,* therefore, are insufficient to protect these rights from encroachment and other forms of usurpation by state and powerful business interests. Existing provisions also do not resolve conflicts with concessions that have already been established within *adat* territories.

- **CBPRs to Customary Forest are qualified with the clause that they must not conflict with "national interests," as interpreted by the state.** This now familiar phrase has long been used since the founding of the Indonesian state to promote government agendas over local community rights (see Chapter II). It needs to be reinterpreted in a more fair and appropriate manner (see Chapter VI).

As this report demonstrates, in fundamental respects these state-centric problems and approaches are not new. Despite the unsustainable degradation of Indonesia's lucrative forests and other natural resources, the state clings to concepts and approaches that originated in the colonial era and were refined during the Suharto dictatorship. Substantive democratic reform and a new understanding of the national interest are long overdue and urgently needed.

Human Rights and Indigenous Peoples

Some progress outside of the natural resource sector in recognizing and protecting the human rights of Indonesians, including indigenous peoples, has taken place in the post-Suharto era. President Wahid released many political prisoners, repealed subversion laws, and apologized for the 1965 massacre of those suspected of involvement with the communist party.[45] He signed the National Human Rights Law No. 39/1999, which contains specific recognition of the government's legal responsibility to protect indigenous peoples' differences, needs, and cultural identity. The law is explicit in calling for recognition of *"community made land rights, in accordance with their development over time,"* (Article 6, Sections 1 and 2; emphasis added).[46]

The first National Congress on Indigenous Peoples was held in Jakarta in 1999. Representatives of indigenous communities throughout the archipelago gathered and demanded legal recognition of their community-based *adat* property rights, and in some especially egregious cases pressed for independent nationhood. Out of the congress, the Alliance of *Adat* Communities (AMAN) was organized as an umbrella network of indigenous communities. AMAN aspires to improve the recognition, participation, and bargaining position of indigenous communities on issues of land rights, forest, and planning on their traditional territories, as well as policy-making in other sectors (Campbell 2001; Fay and Sirait 2001).

The Minister of Agrarian Affairs (which contains the Bureau of Lands, BPN, charged with documenting land titles) attended the National Congress and promised to directly address the problem of *adat* rights in government planning. The BPN later issued the Ministerial Decree on the Resolution of Traditional Rights Conflicts (PerMen BPN 5/1999). This decree authorizes legal titling of *adat* land rights.[47] It recognizes these rights of ownership (*kepunyaan,* not *kemilikan*) as being *communal,* non-transferable, and *private,*[48] characteristics not shared by the management/use right provided for in the Revised Forest Law of 1999. The agrarian affairs decree is a potentially powerful legal tool in favor of legal recognition of private CBPRs, but it has not yet been implemented.

Another potentially useful legal instrument for gaining recognition of indigenous CBPRs in Indonesia is a draft government regulation on customary forests. It could address shortcomings in recent forestry legislation regarding overlapping claims to *adat* forests (Fay and Sirait, personal communication 2001). The draft regulation aims to implement the recognition of *hutan adat,* or customary forests, as provided for in the revised forestry law. It attempts to resolve complicated questions of who will get what rights, and assume what responsibilities, to which resources. The draft defines an *adat* community using criteria taken largely from the precedent of the Krui special status regulation (SK MenHut No.47/1998), which are drawn from colonial concepts of *adat* with the added assumption that communities have remained static under fifty years of intense pressure from states, markets, and social forces (Wignyosoebroto 1999). This includes requiring that:

- The community is still in the form of a unified "association" *(rechtsgemeenschap)* with a common place of residence.
- There are traditional, community-based institutions for controlling forest use.
- There are clear customary law territories recognized by surrounding *adat* communities.
- There are traditional, community-based legal institutions that are functional and complied with by local community members.

- Forest products are still collected to fulfill daily needs, or there are still religious and community relations with the forest (Chapter II, Article 3).

The draft regulation delimits standards of allowable use in customary *adat* forests. Although a determination must be made about what rights are allowed and what responsibilities are associated with these rights, the draft law requires that local communities protect forests from fires and human disturbance. It also requires them to reforest and to pay stumpage fees for any commercial uses (Article 17).

The draft regulation provides a legal mechanism for gaining some degree of tenurial security and protection of CBPRs. Critics, including *adat* leaders, point out several worrisome aspects of the draft (other than those already mentioned with respect to the Revised Forest Law as a whole). First, the decree grants the state an exclusive right to decide whether an *adat* community is in existence and denies the opportunity for revival or hybridization of local communities.[49] Many community leaders and NGOs object that this is not an appropriate role for the state, as it lacks any credible, objective capacity to determine whether an *adat* community is in existence,[50] and is in contravention of the ILO Convention 169 on Indigenous Peoples' Rights that protects the right to self-determination.

Further, *adat* leaders and their NGO supporters are concerned that narrowly defined criteria unilaterally applied by the state through the forest ministry creates new opportunities for corruption and other forms of abuse by external interests coveting *adat* territories. There is enough ambiguity in the draft regulation to create ample potential for state seizure of customary land, and given the decades of bad-faith forest policy, the concerns are not unwarranted. By mandating "government research" to determine the "character, potential and function of the customary forest," (Article 7, Section 2), for example, there is a well-grounded fear that if local communities reveal the potential value of their customary forests, this would only result in their accelerated removal from even de facto community jurisdiction, especially if the forests within their territories are of high timber value. The withdrawal of *adat* status could happen even after recognition is granted, as "community management authority over *hutan adat* may be revoked if it is determined that the *adat* community is no longer in existence or the quality of the forest has declined," (Article 19). Local communities have expressed confusion about the concept of "*adat* territories" used by the state, and object to what they feel is an inappropriate level of involvement of the state in all steps in the recognition process (Fay and Sirait, private interviews, 2001).

Lastly, the draft would oblige an *adat* community to acknowledge, and at least implicitly accept, the government's assertion of state authority over the area. This is a fundamental problem both theoretically and symbolically. Local communities facing immediate threats of displacement and legal usurpation of their CBPRs, however, might find the draft regulation—if it is ever enacted—to be a useful tool. In other words, they may decide that at least in the short term it is better to lease than to lose their *adat* CBPRs as legal recognition can come later.[51]

Negotiating Options for Local Communities within "State Forests"[52]

Based on the Government Regulations (PP) No. 62/1998 and PP 25/2000 on Devolving Certain Tasks to the Local Government, legal responsibility for the delineation of State Forests has been devolved to local governments. The final gazettement, however, remains in the hands of the Minister of Forestry in Jakarta. This devolution requires a revision of the Ministerial Decree on Forest Delineation and the Enclave policy (SK Men 634/1996). Pursuant to this legislation, in September 1998 the Department invited non-governmental participation in a working group tasked to improve departmental procedures for redrawing the boundaries of state forests. NGOs called for the full participation of local people in determining the boundaries and creating community enclaves within the forest zone. Proponents of the legal recognition of *adat* rights joined the working group, because they viewed it as a potentially important opportunity to identify and excise large areas of *adat* territories from so-called "(state-controlled) forest zones."

Predictably, forest department officials resist any reduction in areas considered by them to be State Forest. Nevertheless, the current policies on forest classification, and decentralization of forest planning and delineation (Ministry of Forestry Decrees SK Menhut 32/2001 and SK Menhut 70/2001), are improvements on the 1996 policy. Under the new policy,

- the role of local government in the process of forest delineation would increase significantly, which should result in easier access and greater participation by local people and communities;
- local communities can participate at early stages in the delineation process;
- methods to identify and classify State Forest are no longer based on a scoring system (consideration of rain fall, slope, and type of soil) that was heavily biased towards including almost any area; and
- during the delineation process local communities adjacent to or having claims inside State Forests will be involved in the process of forest planning.

The draft also provides for a process of participation and notification that will determine if the State Forest area is free from third-party (community) claims. This is to precede the placing of permanent markers, thereby making it more difficult for forestry official to ignore local communities.

Community Territorial Enclaves within State Forests

The policy debate on the process of recognizing local community territorial enclaves within areas considered to be State Forests has been going on for some time and at the end of 2001 was still unresolved. The debate centers on what types of prior CBPRs would be recognized by the Department and on how far an enclave should extend. A temporary enclave policy has been recognized by the Department, but in the field the majority of *adat* territories have not yet been enclaved or recognized through Ministerial Decree. Conservative legal staff in the forest ministry take the position that only land covered by Formal Titles (*Sertifikat*) should qualify and only for immediate settlement areas and fixed agriculture in close proximity of settlements. In contrast, *adat* rights proponents on the special working group for implementing Government Regulation (PP) no. 62/ 1998 argue that *hak ulayat*, or customary lands, and not just land areas covered by a *Sertifikat* should be legally recognized as prior rights. They further argue that all *adat* areas, including family-owned agroforestry areas and natural forests within *adat* territories, should be included within an enclave.

Like other forest policy developments during the Reform era, the prospective new enclave policy remains clouded in uncertainty and confusion.

Summary: The Past Not Yet Passed

Many hopeful changes have occurred since the fall of Suharto in 1998. The state has publicly committed itself to democratizing natural resource management. New possibilities have arisen for introducing and amplifying local community voices, including efforts to gain legal recognition or grants of CBPRs to natural resources and community self-governance.

Yet, it seems that New Order and colonial paradigms of the past are not easily swept aside. While new legislation, such as the Revised Forest Law, the National Human Rights Law, and the National Land Board's decree on settling problems concerning customary land rights are important steps towards democratizing access and use of Indonesia's natural resources, they fall far short. To date, they offer no recognition of the past injustices and other ongoing failures in natural resource management. They have not provided legal security for *adat* communities and none at all for mixed or immigrant communities. "Community Forests" (*Hutan Kemasyarakatan*) have been promoted as a means of settling land and resource conflicts, but the concept remains centralized and under state authority. Further, Community Forests have not been sufficiently supported by implementing regulations and laws to make it mainstream forestry practice in Indonesia. The political will and legal mechanisms for implementing democratic reform in the natural resource sectors has been slow to emerge. Until firm legal mechanisms are in place and implemented, the unjust and failed pattern of arbitrary state legal control over natural resources will fester and endure.

Notes

1. Using SPOT remote images, the Center for Remote Imaging, Sensing and Processing (CRISP) calculated burns scars to be 3.0 million ha in Kalimantan; 1.5 million ha in Sumatra during 1997 (Liew et al. 1998); and 2.5 million ha in East Kalimantan in 1998 (Liew personal communication). Some authors (Barber and Sweithelm 2000) cite estimates of over 10 million ha.

2. See Harwell (2000a) for a discussion of the diverse interpretations and implications of the fires disaster of 1997.

3. Formerly Irian Jaya. There are many ethnic groups in Papua, but because of the economic, political, and cultural marginalization since their inclusion into Indonesia in 1969, a new political identity of "Papuan" has emerged (*The Economist*, 14 October 2000; see also Anderson (1987)). A similar process is occurring to politically bind together diverse indigenous groups of Kalimantan as "Dayaks," see Harwell (2000b). For thirty years since its inclusion into Indonesia, Papua was formally designated a Military Operations Area (DOM). Under the DOM, security forces were given a free hand to combat the separatist guerrillas. Although violence was rampant for decades, attacks between separatist guerillas and the military have grown increasingly violent and frequent, beginning just two months after the resignation of Suharto when the military opened fire on 700 demonstrators in Biak who raised the "Morning Star" flag on West Papua (HRW, "Trouble in Irian Jaya," 6 July 1998; "Violence and Political Impasse in Papua" 3 July 2001).

4. Aceh, in the northern tip of Sumatra, has resisted inclusion into Indonesia since the colonial period. Like West Papua, it waged separatist conflict with the military throughout the New Order, which later exploded into protracted violence following the fall of Suharto and the independence of East Timor. (*The Economist* 11 March 2000; Human Rights Watch "Why Aceh is Exploding" 27 August 1999; "The War in Aceh" August 2001).

5. This is not to suggest the lack of violence during the New Order. Indeed, there is ample evidence that the state was involved in sanctioning, fomenting and carrying out violence both in restive outer provinces and in inner Java since the first days of Suharto's rule. See Anderson and McVey (1971); Robinson (1995) for the "counter-coup" that brought Suharto to power and its violent aftermath; Mackie (1974) and Coppel (1983) for anti-Chinese violence of the 1960s and early 70s; Tapol (1983) for Papua; Franke (1981); Dunn (1983) and Ramos Horta (1987) for East Timor; Hefner (2000) for the New Order and Islamic opposition; Peluso and Harwell (2001) in West Kalimantan.

6. On August 30, 1999, the people of East Timor, defying threats and violence by nationalist militias, turned out to vote overwhelmingly for independence. Following the UN-sponsored referendum, the loyalist militias—organized and supported by the Indonesian military—began to terrorize the population, burning the capital city Dili to the ground, killing

more than 1,500 people, and forcing hundreds of thousands across the border into Indonesia, where tens of thousands remain unable to return and continue to be subjected to violence. (*FEER* 16 September 1999, see also numerous reports at http://www.hrw.org).

7. *The Guardian*, 20 July 1998; *International Markets Insight Reports*, 21 October 1998.

8. Among the most notable examples in the natural resources sector are KUDETA (composed of 82 Indonesian NGOs and student organizations), FKKM and FECRC (both made up of NGOs, academics, and reformist government officials. The latter also had members of forest industry).

9. Additional amendments may be enacted by the MPR before 2002.

10. Winters (2001) cites a former bank official's estimate that 30% of Indonesia's World Bank loans went into the pockets of upper level officials. In 2000, the state's auditors found that billions were embezzled during the last years of the Suharto government and that since the "reform" government took over in 1999 some US$20 billion (46% of the years total) had disappeared (*Straits Times*, 18 July 2000).

11. Abbreviated in Bahasa Indonesia simply as KKN, a term that has become popular in the Indonesian vernacular since the end of the New Order.

12. Megawati's party (PDI) had the most votes in the previous general elections (and therefore the most votes in parliament), and her followers rioted in disappointment following her defeat as President. She was elected by the Parliament as Vice-President to Wahid.

13. Jeffrey Winters, Opening Remarks to Conference on Indonesian Human Rights (Indonesian Human Rights Network, 23–25 February, 2001.Washington, DC).

14. Danielle Knight, Inter Press Service report dated October 26, 2001.

15. Tap MPR No. XV/MPR/1998, Decision of Peoples Consultative Assembly of the Republic of Indonesia concerning the implementation of local autonomy; including the arrangement, distribution and equitable utilization of national resources.

16. Promulgation of the implementing regulation PP 25/1999 demonstrated the reluctance of the Ministries of Forestry, and Energy & Mining to relinquish control of the most lucrative permitting.

17. In March 2001, the Minister for Domestic Affairs and Autonomy remarked that the decentralization laws that went into effect on 1 January 2001 might have to be revised as they contain "elements that might contribute

to disintegration" and were unclear about jurisdictions between central, region and district governments (*Media Indonesia* March 13, 2001; *Jakarta Post* 29 August 2001). These revisions were still under heated debate as this book went to press

18. See, e.g., Presidential Decree (Keppres) 10/2001 on the implementation of regional autonomy in the area of land affairs, which confirms that previous regulations and decisions on land affairs are still valid pending the issuance of new regulations.

19. See Bennett (2000a) for some excellent concrete suggestions on how to ensure these new governance structures are accountable to, and representative of, the people.

20. The proximity of power to village life could be interpreted as a means to improve capacity to serve citizen needs and enforce some accountability. Many citizens long for a more responsive and involved state that might live up to its responsibility to protect their interests and help meet their needs. Officials hundreds of miles away are unlikely to be concerned, if even aware, of local discontent. A more cynical interpretation would be that remote officials are less capable of insinuating themselves too far into local affairs, whereas decentralization may increase the likelihood of government interference in and control over everyday life.

21. Contrast this with the MoFEC's own estimates that forestry revenues for 1998 were US$23.7 billion with plantations contributing an additional US$4.1 billion (MoFEC strategic plan for 2001–2005).

22. Danielle Knight, Inter Press Service report dated October 26, 2001. See also Brown (1999). MoFEC officials admit that the amount of illegal logging is almost twice legal logging, and therefore extraction is nearly three times what they estimate to be sustainable.

23. The challenges confronting the effective promotion of CBNRM and the legal recognition of CBPRs with regard to marine and coastal resources are similar in many respects but much less effort has been made in this area. From a bureaucratic perspective, one of the most significant recent developments was the creation of a Ministry of Marine Affairs in late 1999.

24. For more in-depth discussion of recent policy changes, see Fay and Sirait (2001, n.d.); Sirait (n.d.); Sirait et al. (1999); Campbell (2001); Zakaria and Fauzi (2001); Fauzi (2000a, 2000b); Bennett (2000a, 2000b); Tim Kajian Tiga Lembaga (2000); Rahardjo (2000); Colfer et al. (2001).

25. Frequently, advisory boards have been formed to "participate" in institutional and legal reform only to find that their advice and hard work on drafting regulations has been completely disregarded. The Ministry

promulgates its own version of regulations, which provides no real departure from the prevailing paradigms, and on which there was no public consultation. This was particularly the case in the drafting of both the Revised Forestry Law and Government Regulation (PP) 21/1999 (Campbell 2001).

26. One example is PP 25/1999, which is the implementing regulation for the decentralization laws, maintains central ministerial control over most commercial licensing for large-scale forestry and mining concessions. Another is the suggestion that the MoFEC convert all commercial forest enterprises to state-held companies (*perum*) as in Java, rather than subcontracted, as is currently the case in the Outer Islands. This reflects a desire for more centralization, not de-centralization (Bennett 2000b).

27. Fay and Sirait (2001) estimate that 68% of State Forest areas were illegally classified, as they violate procedural requirements to inform and obtain consent of affected communities.

28. For an in-depth look at the development of community rights in forestry, see Sirait (n.d), Fay and Sirait (2001), and Campbell (2001).

29. Some of these generals were given concessions in return for their support of Major General Suharto and as a way of consolidating support for his New Order administration (Barr 1998; see also Ross 2001 and Barber and Talbott 2001).

30. Damar is a resin from the tree *Shorea javanica,* and among others uses, is exported for use as a cosmetic and paint additive.

31. SK MenHut 47/1998 on KDTI. (Fay and Sirait 2001)

32. The groundbreaking 1991 Social Forestry Management Project overseen by GTZ in Sanggau, West Kalimantan was different in that it was indeed a devolution of authority by the forestry ministry, but not to an indigenous management authority.

33. Since the fall of Suharto, farmers have begun to push for recognition of their ownership rights. See Wrangham (2001), AMAN Congress of Indigenous Peoples, and Chapter IV of this volume.

34. See Fay et al. (2000); Campbell (2001). See community agreements in Chapter IV of this volume.

35. At a time when the thirty-five year leases on large concessions have been re-examined (under IMF pressure) as not contributing to sustainable management since they do not allow enough time for a second cut, a thirty-five year permit raises concerns about potential impacts on forest cover.

36. SK Menhutbun 677/98, revised through SK Menhutbun 865/99.

37. The government's Five Year Plan for 2001–2005 (Propenas, or Program Pembangunan Nasional) mandates the development of community forestry

(Hutan Kemasyarakatan and Hutan Rakyat dan Perkebunan) programs in order to increase community participation and initiative in forest development (Chapter IV, section G). Further, the National Legal Guidelines (GBHN) for 1999–2004 specifically mandate the "development of land policy to increase the just, transparent, and productive access and enjoyment of benefits, prioritizing community rights including traditional rights (*hak ulayat*) in order to achieve more balanced and compatible regional planning," (from Sirait n.d.).

38. The 1998 Minister for Forestry and Estate Crops established a Reform Committee (FECRC), composed of academics, NGOs, industry representatives, and forestry officials. This committee was to assist in charting a new vision for forest management, including ministry restructuring and drafting new legislation. Like FKKM, which had also been invited to participate in the drafting of new forest laws, FECRC was caught by surprise when the Ministry independently promulgated its own version of the new Forestry Law (UU41/1999) and the new Government Regulation on production regulations (PP 6/1999). These developments are described in more detail by Campbell (2001) and Fay and Sirait (2001).

39. As evidenced by PP6/199 and SK MenHutBun 677/1998, which expand some opportunities for limited commercial participation but only recognize collection rights, not ownership.

40. Revised Forestry Law 41/1999, SK MenHutBun 677/1998, PP 6/1999, SK 31/ 2001.

41. The law disregards the fact that many local community experiences with co-ops have not been positive. The state-run village cooperatives, or Kooperasi Unit Desa (KUD), are known as being largely controlled by village elites and are therefore poor models of "cooperation"—a fact that has fostered distrust of the concept.

42. Article 67 states that "Customary communities are recognized if they truly embody elements such as the following: the community is still in the form of an association (*rechtsgemeenschap*); there are institutions in the form of customary control apparatus; there are clear customary law regions; there are legal institutions, specifically a customary judicature, that are obeyed; and forest products are still collected from the surrounding forest regions to fulfill daily needs."

43. "…as a consequence of the State's right to control and manage as the organization of authority over the people under the principle of the Unitary State of the Republic of Indonesia." Elucidation of Paragraph VII of Considerations.

44. Rights of traditional law communities (*masyarakat hukum adat*) are allowed "as long as that community still exists and is recognized [by the local government regulations] as such," (Article 5, Section 3; emphasis added). This presents an unreasonable requirement for local communities: in order to be recognized they must already be recognized (Campbell 2001). Section 4 goes on to state "if the customary community no longer exists, the right to manage the customary forest reverts to the government." See discussion on the Draft Adat Decree for more details on these criteria.

45. Many argue that these advances are largely symbolic, since any real progress was confounded by Wahid's political compromises. Likewise, the brutal reign of terror that leveled East Timor following the vote for independence cast a pall over the "reform" cabinet of Wahid and then head of Armed Forces, General Wiranto.

46. This responsibility was also mandated in the Decision of the People's Consultative Assembly (Tap MPR) on Human Rights No. XVII/MPR/1999, Article 41.

47. To be done by regional government. This legislation is weakened under decentralization because Ministerial Decrees are now subordinate to regional regulations (*perda*).

48. Note that "private" is not synonymous with individual title, but rather indicates its status as outside of government control ("public"). While the right is non-transferable, this regulation allows communities to lease their land to the government, who can then transfer this lease to private companies.

49. *Adat* communities determined to be no longer in existence may not be revived (Article 6, Section 3).

50. These valid critiques are aside from the logistical observation that local governments are simply incapable of this amount of careful research, especially given their recently expanded administrative load under decentralization.

51. Similar concerns in the Philippines prompted some threatened indigenous communities in the 1980s and early 1990s to lease their ancestral domains. Most of these communities are expected to convert their leases into Certificates of Ancestral Titles (CADTs) under the Indigenous Peoples Rights Act of 1997.

52. The section draws in detail from "Reforming the Reformists: Challenges to Government Forestry Reform in Post-Suharto Indonesia" (Fay and Sirait 2001).

VI.

TOWARDS A NEW PARADIGM OF ENVIRONMENTAL JUSTICE AND THE NATIONAL INTEREST

The post-Suharto era has been marked by new legislation and constitutional reforms, including the restructuring of various state functions and approaches. Many rhetorical commitments have been made by government officials to democratize access to Indonesia's natural resources. Legislation in the environmental and natural resource sectors, however, continues to lag far behind promising community and NGO initiatives currently underway on the ground. This lag has resulted in an emerging policy vacuum, as described in Chapter IV, in which an increasing number of innovative management agreements are being negotiated between local communities and government officials, and/or concessionaires.

Daily conflicts over natural resources are still by far the more common reality confronting millions of rural Indonesian citizens directly dependent on natural resources. These conflicts manifest the persistent tendency of Indonesian national laws and policies to rely on unjust legal premises that originated in the colonial era and overlook the aspirations, rights, problems, and contributions of rural citizens. Whether traditional or migrant, rural communities throughout Indonesia remain largely voiceless in law and policy-making processes that directly impact their lives and livelihoods, including their CBPRs. Nevertheless, the tumultuous political developments of recent years have contributed to widespread support for reform. There is an unprecedented opportunity to break past legal legacies and to promote environmental justice and wise management of Indonesia's vast natural resources.

Whose Development? Whose Common Good?

Over the past decades in Indonesia and in many other countries, advocacy on behalf of rural natural resource users has too often been incorrectly perceived as pitting local interests against the national interest. This enduring misperception has been used effectively by those who benefit from Indonesia's prevailing legal interpretations to monopolize access to and control over much of the nation's natural resources. Ostensibly, this control has been used to generate domestic capital to finance national development, and in some instances, this has been done. A much more common outcome, however, has been the self-serving enrichment of a powerful and politically connected minority at the expense of the nation's impoverished majority.

All citizens of Indonesia have legal rights and are entitled to look to the state as an ally in promoting their well being and basic needs, regardless of their ethnic, educational, and financial status. Rural people directly dependent on natural resources still constitute a majority of Indonesia's citizens, yet their voices are largely unheard in official decision-making processes regarding the use and allocation of legal rights to natural resources. It is simply not credible anymore to claim that it is in the national interest for most benefits to flow to a relatively few urban commercial enterprises who are given priority over the welfare of the national majority.

This report provides evidence and analysis from various sources throughout Indonesia that demonstrate enduring support for and benefits from traditional and other types of community-based natural resource management (CBNRM) initiatives and institutions. The evidence is also clear and convincing that the current, official approach favoring large-scale commercial resource extraction and exploitation by external actors, with no accountability to locally affected citizens, is unsustainable and not in the national interest. A broader, more encompassing and fair definition of Indonesia's national interest, including social development and the principles of a unitary state, would not result in widespread arbitrary displacements and other unjust treatment of rural constituencies directly dependent on natural resources.

The case studies, local agreements, and contemporary literature that are referenced in this report highlight the existence, and innovative and dynamic nature, of local community-based institutions for natural resource management and governance. They underscore the negative influence that existing national laws and policies have on the development, function, and viability of local, community-based institutions and rights. These laws and policies endure in a policy environment that still largely fosters undemocratic, unaccountable, and unrepresentative state governance.

Towards a New Paradigm of Environmental Justice

The fundamental issue addressed in this report is whether the citizens who are most directly impacted by government-supported natural resource development and conservation initiatives should be expected to bear the highest costs and receive the lowest benefits, or in many cases no benefits at all. Simply stated, this report's fundamental conclusion is that Indonesia's common good can best be promoted by the enactment and implementation of national laws and policies that ensure local communities are meaningfully able to participate in and benefit from official natural-resource-management initiatives.

Helping the majority of Indonesia's citizens to improve their welfare and livelihoods; maintain their food security; and preserve their communities, cultural traditions, local institutions, and economies is in the nation's best interest. An official approach supportive of community-based management would help to foster and maintain local incentives for conservation and sustainable management. It would also provide that the well-being of the majority of Indonesian citizens is included in the official definition of the national interest.

Rather than promoting sustainable development, including local and national well-being, long-established prevailing interpretations of national laws and policies effectively promote a type of unjust and environmentally unwise official control over local community affairs. They render many rural citizens vulnerable to arbitrary and unjust interpretations of government officials and commercial entrepreneurs. An "institutional culture" that adheres to narrow policy interpretations by top-down bureaucracies restricts the flexibility of field officers to recognize and incorporate valuable local practice and knowledge (case study by Safitri). A democratic solution is not to narrow the options for governmental officials in the field. Rather, it would be to ensure the accountability, transparency and flexibility of official decision-making processes so that local community members have voice, recourse, and incentives to benefit from their investments of knowledge, time and labor.

It merits emphasizing that this report does not present or promote any romanticized descriptions of "tradition" or "timeless ecological harmony." Obviously, not all traditional and local communities are democratic, homogenous, or harmonious. Nor are all CBPRs or local practices environmentally harmless or sustainable. Like human beings elsewhere, rural people in Indonesia often lack access to important knowledge and other resources. They weigh both personal as well as communal costs and benefits when making decisions that involve use of their time, labor, and natural resources. In some instances, traditional practices that were once sustainable may no longer be appropriate. Under increasing demographic, political, and market pressures, cooperation and sustainable use sometimes have given way to competitive self-interests, and this can result in inequitable access and degradation of natural resources. The influx of outsiders unaware of or unconcerned about local community norms and traditions can also weaken and undermine sustainable local practices, as can unwise and unfair state laws and regulations.

Rather than portraying local community institutions and rights as a timeless panacea, this report highlights the importance of supporting flexible and accountable CBNRM initiatives. Often, this can best occur in collaboration with accountable and responsive government officials. The real issue is not whether there is a role for government. The question is how the role of government can evolve to ensure that local people have legal incentives and support for sustainable natural resource management and conservation. This requires legal guarantees for substantive participation and benefit sharing, and ensuring that their voices are heard and their concerns and rights are addressed.

What then is the role of external regulation in situations where local communities have recognized legal rights, including primary management authority over local natural resources? How does that role differ in places where local communities are managing natural resources sustainably?

Under conditions of changing markets and population pressures, this report has identified that key interface conditions between external authorities and local communities should include:

- Legal recognition of private community-based *adat* property rights, and granting of management rights for non-*adat* communities, including support for improved defense from external encroachment and unsustainable exploitation.
- Efforts to support local institutions that are representative and accountable.
- Meaningful and transparent access to legal and technical information and resources, including equitable dispute mediation processes.
- Strengthening of community-based enforcement and monitoring capabilities.
- Reciprocal arrangements (including financial and other benefits) for environmental services maintained and protected by local communities.

Reinterpreting the Indonesian Constitution: Articles 18 and 33

As highlighted throughout this report, under both the New and post–New Order administrations' laws and policies, the natural resource sector can be characterized by fundamental tensions between centralized state control and community-based governance, with the state being dominant. Meanwhile, in many regions of Indonesia, inattention to community-based institutions and CBPRs is endangering the national interest by damaging local welfare and environmental assets. It generates ill will towards the government and threatens national solidarity. It also saps, and in some cases has destroyed, the positive contributions made by local communities to the national economy and to protecting the natural environment. There are no more tragic examples than the chronic and still unresolved regional conflicts in Aceh, Kalimantan, Papua and elsewhere.

Powerful legal support for a new approach that, if implemented, would promote substantive democracy, environmental justice, and popular support for national unity can be found in the Indonesian Constitution. In many nations, including the United States, with the world's oldest written constitution, which has endured for over two centuries, the founding document is often reinterpreted with regards to history, new knowledge and evolving contemporary events. In light of decades of exploitation and abuse of local rural communities under the imprimatur of the Indonesian state, a historically informed, more just and culturally respectful reinterpretation of Indonesia's constitutional mandates is urgently needed.

The Indonesian constitution and subsequent laws obligate the state to protect local welfare and promote the sustainable management of its natural resources for the maximum benefit of all citizens. There is no qualification. All Indonesian citizens are to reap benefits from national development, including those far from urban centers.

The clearest expression of this mandate is in Article 18 of the Indonesian Constitution. Pursuant to Article 18, Indonesia has been constitutionally considered to be a united but diverse nation. Implicit in this is recognition of the importance and legitimacy of legal pluralism.[1]

Until it was amended in August 2000, Article 18 provided that

> [T]he division of the territory of Indonesia into large and small regions shall be prescribed by law in consideration of and with due regard to the principles of deliberation in the government system and the hereditary rights of special territories.

This provision, at minimum, mandated the Indonesian state to draw from and build upon indigenous institutions that in many cases predated and endured during the colonial era. It specifically recognized both the diversity and authority of local communities in what are historically known as "special areas" (*daerah istimewa*). These areas are known to have unique institutions and hereditary rights. As such for over a half century, Article 18 mandated the Indonesian state to protect the nation's indigenous cultural heritage and rights, a mandate that was in most respects ignored.

As amended in August 2000, Article 18 (b) (2) now provides that

> [T]he state shall acknowledge and respect traditional societies along with their customary rights as long as these remain in existence and are in accordance with the societal development and the principles of the Unitary State of the Republic of Indonesia, and shall be regulated by law.

Whether customary or hereditary, Article 18 clearly acknowledges the existence of community-based rights that originated autonomously from the Indonesian state, whether colonial or post-colonial.

Article 18 manifests one side of a longstanding inherent tension in the Indonesian Constitution between community-based *adat* rights and state control. Article 33 manifests the other side. Since Indonesia's independence in 1945, this tension has been resolved almost by rote in favor of Article 33, which has long been accorded much more attention and weight than Article 18.

Article 33 provides that "the land, water and their natural riches are controlled by the state." This article was intended to prohibit foreign control of Indonesia's natural riches and thereby provide for the well-being of the new nation as a whole. However well intentioned its drafters may have been, this provision in Article 33 nevertheless echoes its colonial precedent of state primacy, the Dutch colonial *Domeinverklaring* or Domain Declarations. It has served as legal justification for sweeping state control (see Chapter II, Independence, *Adat* and the Constitution).

Significantly, Article 33 does not assert state ownership. Rather it mandates that state control is to be used for the "maximum prosperity (or greatest benefit) of the people" (Section 3). This is consistent with Roman law concepts distinguishing *imperium* from *dominium*.[2] *Imperium* refers to state sovereignty, and in most parts of Indonesia, local communities are not clamoring to break away from the Indonesian state. Rather they aspire for more *dominium*, or management authority over the natural resources that they directly depend on for their lives and livelihoods. As emphasized in Chapter I, legal recognition of private *adat* CBPRs would not preclude the state from exercising its powers of eminent domain over the nation, provided the power is used in the public interest as defined in a broad and inclusive manner. Instead, it would, among other things, prevent the state from arbitrary and unjust usurpations of local rights.

For most rural Indonesians, and arguably the nation as a whole, the constitutional mandate in Article 33 to promote the common good has been systematically overlooked in New Order legislation and implementation (Moniaga 1993). Indeed, the research relied on in this report almost uniformly demonstrates that the Indonesian state has consistently failed to manage natural resources for the maximum prosperity of all of its citizens.[3] In light of the many tragic experiences endured by rural people during Indonesia's first half century of independence, and the overlooked mandates of Article 18, what democratic justification remains for continuing this failed approach?

The major challenge in reinterpreting Indonesia's constitution with regard to natural resources, including the recent amendments, will likely revolve around differing concepts of social development and the principles of a unitary state. In most areas of Indonesia, however, neither concept can reasonably preclude legal recognition of private community-based *adat* property rights and institutions. Rather, in light of Indonesia's history, these concepts mandate recognition more than ever before.

Indonesia's transition from a colony to a republic resulted in little change in state laws, policies, and practices for allocating power and wealth among the nation's rural peoples. With regard to natural resources, the new republic largely mirrored the policies and designs of the former colonial government. Many political and economic elites who profited under the auspices of the Dutch colonial state continued to profit, in an uninterrupted manner, under the auspices of the Indonesian Republic. More importantly, the politically and economically disenfranchised majority of Indonesians living in poverty continue to be substantively marginalized in national laws and policies.

After more than half a century of political independence, the substantive continuity between the colonial and politically independent Indonesian state remains strong, especially in terms of laws and policies concerning property rights and natural resources. This raises a host of questions. Perhaps foremost is the question of when, if ever, there was any substantive democratic reconstitution of the Indonesian state that genuinely considered and reflected the aspirations, rights, and potentials of the entire citizenry, especially the impoverished rural majority.

Reinterpreting Article 18 as having precedence over Article 33 would honorably answer the question. It would require that natural resources covered by *adat* rights be recognized as privately owned by local communities and not merely as specially classified state-owned areas.[4] This would contribute to the building of a grander and more inclusive republic in partnership with all citizens, especially the most vulnerable. Success would herald the emergence of a substantive democracy and a sense of respect that could solidify national unity and purpose throughout Indonesia's far-flung regions.

On-the-Ground Delineation of State Lands

A necessary step in pursing a more just, inclusive, and sustainable approach to rural Indonesians directly dependent on natural resources includes addressing the ubiquitous and growing conflicts over so-called "state land." Indonesia is covered by millions of hectares of *adat* CBPRs, including coastal and marine resources, agroforests, and managed natural stands.[5] Millions more hectares are covered by more recently established community-based claims by migrants. Far from idle or unproductive, many of these areas contribute significantly to the national economy. They provide approximately 70% of rubber, at least 80% of the damar resin, approximately 80 to 90% of marketed fruits, and significant quantities of the tree-crop exports cinnamon, clove, nutmeg, coffee, and candlenut (de Foresta and Michon 1997). Rattan canes from smallholder-tended gardens had an export value of US$360 million in 1994 (De Berr and MacDermott 1996). In Sumatra alone, about 4 million ha have been converted by local people into various kinds of agroforests without any outside assistance (de Foresta and Michon 1993). An estimated 7 million people in Sumatra and Kalimantan are living off agroforests consisting or rubber trees that spread across approximately 2.5 million ha.[6]

The largest areas claimed by the state are within the so-called State Forest Zone. These vast areas must be re-evaluated and classified or reclassified with the full participation of local people, a process that would be in accordance with Article 18 of the Constitution. There are other legal reasons as well for ensuring more democratic and participatory processes.

First, the government's own data reveal that approximately two-thirds of the area the Department of Forestry claims as State Forest Zone has yet to be legally gazetted. The legal gazettement of the State Forest Zone is contingent on notification units (BATB) being signed by the Minister of Forestry. As of February 1999, of the 2531 units identified during the 1984 classification process, only 1719 units have been signed, leaving 812 units still unfinished (INTAG n.d.; cited in Fay and Sirait 1999). As a result, by the government's own admission, only 68% of what the ministry considers "the state forest zone" is legally under its putative jurisdiction. Further, since the subsequent provincial, district, and "harmonized" (*paduserasi*) forest planning processes, it is even more urgent that the lands under state jurisdiction be examined for procedural violations.

Second, the implementation of previous delineation processes calls into question the legality of even this remaining ungazetted portion. Information as to which areas have been formally gazetted (as required by law) is unavailable to local communities. Forest boundary delineation and gazettement procedures require that all local communities be informed of the creation of State Forest in their areas, and community leaders must sign documents saying they were informed and that there were no outstanding rights to the area. It is widely known that many areas were gazetted by the forestry ministry in violation of this requirement.[7]

Finally, the new forest law clearly defines State Forest as "a forest located on lands unencumbered by rights (*tidak dibebani hak atas tanah*)," (Revised Basic Forestry Law, Article 1, Section 4; also MoFEC Decree (SK) No. 32/2000, Article 5, Section 2, Paragraph b).[8] Using these definitions it is clear that only a fraction of the lands classified as State Forest actually qualify as such. This definition of the State Forest offers a critical entry point for resolving conflicts between local communities, the government, and concessionaires.

There is an important related need for the government of Indonesia to reassess the methods used by the Department of Forestry to more precisely define the State Forest Zone. It is well accepted that the state's definition of the forest estate includes areas covered by CBPRs. This has led to widespread and increasing conflict on the ground between local people and forest industries.[9]

Further, at the National Conference on Natural Resources on May 23, 2000, former President Wahid himself made the following important points.

- *Adat* communities are weak because they have been intentionally weakened so that the state and business sector can be strong. Therefore *adat* communities must be heard, including their declaration that *adat* communities are the legal owners of natural resources (provided that they prove themselves to be willing to dialogue and negotiate with other stakeholders).

- With respect to natural resources, the state is only a management advisor and mediator of good negotiation processes.
- The government has a plan to return 40% of state-owned estate crops to the public, including the *adat* community, either in the form of land holdings or shares in the estates. This is based on the historical conditions under which the land was appropriated illegally and without compensation.[10]

These comments signaled a clear public commitment to reassess forest classifications and to recognize rights that were ignored during the process of State Forest designation. Hopefully the new administration of President Sukarnoputri will follow through with these commitments.

The legal and policy mechanisms for what can be described as land reform in the forest zone already exist and could perhaps be allied in coastal and marine areas as well. Three priorities for forest reform were recently discussed at a one-day seminar concerning tenure rights issues inside the State Forest Zone and the government of Indonesia's commitment before the Consultative Group on Indonesia to address this problem.[11]

The priorities begin with a rationalization process that would more accurately and legally determine which areas should be State Forest; second is the development of guidelines to recognize *adat* rights; and third is the refinement of stewardship or management agreements with community-based institutions, primarily migrant farming inside the State Forest Zone. If implemented, the first priority would naturally pave the way for the other two. It is based on the wide recognition that the basis for determining State Forest areas, as well as the procedures, is deeply flawed. This is most evident in the Revised Forest Law of 1999 that defines forest as

- "a unit of ecosystem in the form of land comprising biological resources, dominated by trees in their *natural forms* and environment, which cannot be separated from each other" (emphasis added);

- "a certain area is designated or stipulated by government to be retained as permanent forest"; and
- "a forest located on lands unencumbered by other rights."

Using these definitions, it is clear that only a fraction of the lands classified as State Forest actually qualify as such. It is well documented that Indonesia is covered by millions of hectares of community forests and individually owned agroforests, and therefore large areas of what the MoFEC classifies as natural forest, is in fact claimed by farmers as private land.[12] Given that most of these community-based agroforestry systems are misclassified as State Forest, should they be reclassified as private lands, it is not difficult to envision a State Forest Zone that is close to half of the current 143 million hectares.

Not by *Adat* Alone

While there are clear legal precedents for recognizing community-based *adat* property rights, this report does not conclude that only *adat* institutions should be the beneficiaries of reforms in natural resource management. Many communities have long innovated on tradition (or wish to now do so), which in some cases might have been highly stratified and undemocratic, to devise hybrid forms of governance. In such situations, each community should be given the opportunity to form their own institutions for managing natural resources. Further, many communities are mixed or immigrant or may have been highly mobile and therefore have no clear-cut *adat* rights to territory. Community management agreements on lands in the "state forest" zone based on the "special use" or *hutan desa* (village forest) areas are now being experimented with in Lampung, Southern Sumatra; Kutai, East Kalimantan; and Wonosobo, Central Java and other areas (Sirait, personal communication, September 30, 2001). From a social justice perspective, it is clear that laws and policies for "legalizing" these diverse kinds of arrangements need to be developed to accommodate the full spectrum of natural resource-dependent communities.

Solutions lie not only in recognition of *adat* community rights, but also in creatively forging new arrangements for non-*adat* and mixed communities, who in many locales are the most disadvantaged.

For example, in contrast to *adat* communities with strong local institutions and tacit recognition of community-based rights, in Lampung, Sumatra, the relationship between the community and the state was even more imbalanced (case study by Safitri). Residents were immigrants from Central and East Java, although many had come as laborers half a century ago during the colonial period to work on plantations.

In 1986, an area known as Gunung Betung was declared to be a Protected Forest. All residents were relocated without compensation, because they were considered by the government to be illegal squatters who had no rights and who were deemed incapable of protecting the forest. Ever since, the community's weak bargaining position has pervaded interactions with the forestry officials and has increased bitterness and distrust. Local people who plant in or collect from the Protected Forest must pay expensive bribes to the forest guards in exchange for not being sanctioned for their "illegal" activity. Forest guards have refused to act as mediators if local produce (fruits, fodder, fiber, or timber, etc.) is stolen, because they consider any planting or harvesting in the forest to be illegal and all local claims to be null and void. A condition of open access in the protected area was thereby effectively created, as there were no legally recognized and secure property rights.

In response, mediators from the University of Indonesia (UI) and UI-Lampung helped local communities to form a Forest Management and Conservation Group, made up of 123 representatives of six villages. The representatives decided that if the state would not protect the resources, local communities should band together cooperatively to manage the forest for everyone's benefit. They formalized a cooperative agreement regarding their local rights and responsibilities and developed implementing regulations.[13] According to the agreement, individuals of the member villages are entitled to

- exclusive rights to harvest products of their planted and tended plants;
- help with mediation of disputes;
- protection from any outside threats related to forest management; and

- have their suggestions and opinions respectfully heard in group meetings.

The agreement, however, did not only entail government concessions. In return, local community members agreed to
- plant perennials only in their own gardens and not attempt to stake claims elsewhere;
- not open new gardens, extend old gardens, or fell trees;
- not fell trees at any time without notification and approval from the group;
- take only as much fodder as one can carry in one backpack per day;
- not steal or accept stolen produce from someone else's garden;
- help stop theft of forest products by reporting or apprehending thieves; and
- help to prevent and extinguish all forest fires.

A schedule of graduated sanctions was drawn up according to the seriousness of the offense and the number of repeated violations. The sanctions include warnings, confiscation of stolen goods, fines, and the use of formal legal prosecution. To reduce the potential for obstruction, the rules and sanctions were presented to the local district official for approval. Although many challenges remain, this case is another demonstration that both indigenous and migrant communities have incentives and capacities to form viable cooperative management institutions that are in the national interest.

Innovative Opportunities to Link Community-Based Property Rights and Conservation

As highlighted throughout this report, millions of hectares of Indonesia are already being managed by local people with little or no assistance or recognition from government. In areas that are valued for conservation of biodiversity and carbon sinks, or for their ecosystem functions, however, a different bundle of state incentives are needed to protect rather than extract natural resources (see, e.g., Gullison et al. 2000; Ferraro 2001; Smith and Scherr n.d.). Rather than expecting local communities (and local governments) to protect natural resources that many in Indonesia and the international community value, and to do this for free, innovative incentives (both monetary and in-kind) could act as "easements" to offset the opportunity costs of foregoing the commercial extraction of timber and other natural resources. While communities are not flawless managers, when provided with proper incentives and checks and balances, many have the ability to protect the natural resources in which their future, present, and past are so deeply intertwined.

The urgency for preventing and reversing the deterioration of local livelihoods is not justified exclusively by a humanitarian concern for resource-dependent people. Many communities in Indonesia manage landscapes that provide environmental services to outside beneficiaries but without legally sharing in the benefits of those services. The services include clean and abundant water supplies from watersheds, biodiversity protection, and stocks of carbon that may alleviate global climate change.

Rewarding local communities for providing these services would enhance their livelihoods and reduce poverty. Clear opportunities are now emerging in this respect. Many of the current successes (e.g., in Malaysia, Costa Rica, Colombia, Venezuela, Chile, Guyana, and Peru) in environmental transfer payments, however, have only benefited states, large landowners, and concessionaires. Rather than recognizing and providing compensation to local communities for conservation and other natural resource management activities already being undertaken by communities, some payments have effectively resulted in their displacement (Smith and Scherr n.d.). This is also potentially true for emerging interest in trading in carbon sequestration credits.[14] The objective should be to ensure that some of the potential benefits offered by transfer payments are channeled to the local communities that provide the services.

Recognition of local rights is necessary but by itself is insufficient for ensuring sustainable CBNRM. New legal tools will require clear implementing regulations that provide for participatory and proper enforcement and dispute-processing mechanisms; emphasize that commercial timber production is not the only possible management goal; and ensure local control over the form and development of community institutions.

A fundamental shift in orientation towards democratizing access to forests, minerals, and coastal and marine resources is needed. This requires a flexible and multi-pronged approach. The correct starting point would be legally recognizing *adat* CBPRs, and thereby formally privatizing millions of hectares that are owned by local communities and cannot justifiably be classified as (public) State Forest. By doing this, the Ministry of Forestry would become a positive force in Indonesia's efforts to remake the nation and advance in a positive and progressive manner toward national reconciliation.

Notes

1. See Chapter II for more background information on the drafting of the 1945 constitution.

2. See Maine (1987).

3. This fact is not unique to Indonesia. Evidence of the failure of exclusive state management is now conclusive from many parts of the world. For example, see Lynch (1990).

4. The Revised Forest Law of 1999 provides for recognition of *adat* forest areas within the State Forest (Chapter II, Article 5(2)). Although this provision is an unprecedented and welcome step towards recognizing community-based *adat* rights, it fails to recognize that *adat* areas are community-owned.

5. For the most comprehensive publication to date on community-created forests see de Foresta et al. (2001).

6. See Fay and de Foresta (1998).

7. This final section relies heavily on "Getting the Boundaries Right: Indonesia's Urgent Need to Redefine its Forest Estate," (Fay and Sirait 1999).

8. Note that the article does *not* use the word *milik,* which specifically indicates "ownership" (which is commonly understood to indicate individual titled rights), but rather an unqualified *hak,* which refers to the broader idea of "rights."

9. See Chapter III of this volume; Bachriadi n.d. In addition, The Consortium for Supporting Community-Based Forest System Management (KPSHK) cites as many as 19,492 cases of conflict from 1990-1999 between local communities and the state or concessionaires (see Muhsi 2000).

10. Reported by Ahmad (2000).

11. The CGI is an international bilateral and multilateral donor forum led by the World Bank. These recommendations were presented by ICRAF and partners at a seminar at the Department of Forestry on May 24, 2001.

12. de Foresta and Kusworo (forthcoming).

13. See also Chapter IV for more examples of local initiatives in crafting agreements with other villages, local government, or industry. These local innovations are already underway, ahead of formal legal arrangements, and should be seen as precedents for possibilities for working out conflicts between communities and the state, as well as parastatal entities such as plantations and other concessionaires.

14. To assure that the rights of indigenous and other local communities are protected and that the Clean Development Mechanism (CDM) of the Climate Change Convention (CCC) is sustainable, equitable, and successful, a meeting was held for representatives of indigenous and other local communities who may be affected by implementation of the CDM. The meeting took place in Quito, Ecuador in May 2000 and was attended by representatives from Kenya, South Africa, the Philippines, and Indonesia, as well as several Latin American countries. More information on the workshop, including the text of the Quito Declaration made there, can be viewed on CIEL's Web site at: <www.ciel.org.> See also Smith and Schell (n.d).

CONCLUSION

Since the fall of President Suharto in May 1998, legal developments in Indonesia have been unfolding in an extraordinarily fluid and unstable environment. Despite enormous problems facing the government since the inauguration of President Wahid in October 1999 and President Sukarnoputri in August 2001, in many respects Indonesia seems to be moving in positive directions. The more democratic and transparent character of the new governments has had discernible and positive impacts on efforts to reform Indonesia's natural resource laws, policies, and practices

As this report has shown, the failure of Indonesia's laws, policies, and management practices to protect natural resources and improve the welfare of rural citizens is increasingly acknowledged, even by the government itself. This acknowledgment includes a growing consensus among policy analysts that what drives the forest and mining ministries is the desire to maintain control over as much of Indonesia's natural resources as possible. When opportunities to profit from the logging of natural forests end in the near future, the control of land for timber plantations and reforestation projects will intensify even more and become the main arena for rent-seeking activities.

In Indonesia as elsewhere, the transition to democracy is a complicated and controversial process, and attention to regional and local variations, rather than generalized programs, is critical. "Getting the institutions right" is a dynamic process that assumes that, given proper incentives, local users are neither homogenous nor helpless, but are capable of great flexibility and initiative in adapting to resource dilemmas (Ostrom 1990). The key is not to assign uniform, state-imposed standards on local communities that they cannot possibly live up to (and which are more stringent than those applied to large commercial concessionaires), nor to use national law to remove natural resources from local control and livelihoods.

Rather, solutions lie in removing legal disincentives for and providing legal support for community-based institutions, rights, and initiatives. In other words, the state should consider not what it can *give* to communities, but what it can *stop taking away* (Dove 1993a, 1998).

Summary of Key Recommendations

The key recommendations reiterated below are based upon case studies, BSP KEMALA technical reports and other field research and policy analysis from throughout Indonesia. They are specific suggestions for implementing a just and democratic paradigm for conservation and natural resource management in Indonesia. Such a new paradigm would include legal recognition of community-based *adat* property rights and would contribute to conservation and sustainable development on local, regional and national levels.

- Legally recognize and support traditional adat laws concerning natural resources, including community-based adat property rights (CBPRs) to land, forests, marine and coastal resources.
- The positive contributions of indigenous and other local communities in managing natural resources should be acknowledged and supported in official natural resources planning and implementation processes.
- Indigenous and other local communities directly dependent on natural resources should be the principle partners in government-sponsored conservation and natural resource management initiatives.
- Since in most cases legal documents are lacking, locally appropriate forms of evidence, e.g., fallow fields, gravesites, orchards, and oral histories, should be sufficient to prove indigenous ownership.
- Sufficient evidence of indigenous *adat* ownership should create a legal presumption that areas where the evidence cannot be classified or used for commercial exploitation or other uses without the prior informed consent of local citizens whose property rights would be affected.
- Local migrant communities should be provided meaningful opportunities to acquire legal rights to manage natural resources they directly depend on for their lives and livelihoods.

- State institutions responsible for issuing tenure instruments to local communities should not have authority to make unilateral and arbitrary determinations. All official decision-making processes concerning natural resources should be transparent and participatory.
- The issuance of any tenure instruments to local communities should not be preconditioned on enterprise development, and should also not preclude such development.
- The legal recognition or grant of community rights should be treated separately from enterprise development so problems such as inadequate cash flow and financial losses do not result in the revocation of local community rights.
- State sponsored enterprise development initiatives should ensure benefits to all local community members and not compromise subsistence resource uses.
- In order to equitably address local boundary conflicts, transparent dispute management processes are needed. Training in conflict mediation should be provided to local communities and governments and NGO actors.
- Government should provide technical support, public access to information, and support for local monitoring and enforcement.
- Training of local officials is needed to increase their capacities to understand and respond to local needs and concerns.

There are indications of renewed interest in and hope for Indonesian legal processes. The corrupting influences of the decades-long Suharto regime are being challenged on various levels. Law in Indonesia has for many decades been used as a tool of the powerful against the weak. Now law is increasingly being viewed as a key tool for meaningful and sustained reform. These developments, however, are relatively nascent and fragile. Much depends on how the national government manages and responds to pressures for reform. Nevertheless, on balance, as of January 2002, the prospects for democratic reform appear much more hopeful than could have been imagined just a few years ago.

About the Authors

Emily E. Harwell is a Finberg Research Fellow in the Asia Division of Human Rights Watch, where she is documenting cases linking environmental and human rights abuses. She earned her Ph.D. in December 2000 from the Yale School of Forestry and Environmental Studies. Her dissertation examines the historical dynamics of ethnic identity, territory, and resource conflicts in the Danau Sentarum lakes region of West Kalimantan, Indonesia. She has been studying resource politics in Indonesia since 1994.

Owen J. Lynch is a senior attorney and managing director of the Law and Communities Program at the Center for International Environmental Law (CIEL) in Washington, DC. For more than two decades, he has been has been actively engaged in fostering public interest law careers in Asia and more recently Africa, the Pacific and Latin America. He taught for eight years (1981–1988) at the University of the Philippines College of Law. Owen's substantive focus is on human rights and sustainable development issues, especially community-based property rights (CBPRs) and their legal recognition in national and international laws.

Owen received Master of Laws and Doctor of Laws degrees from Yale University in 1985 and 1992. His doctoral dissertation, "Colonial Legacies in a Fragile Republic: A History of Philippine Land Law and State Formation with Emphasis on the Early U.S. Regime (1898–1913)," was awarded the Ambrose Gherini Prize for best work on an international law topic at Yale University in 1992.

LITERATURE CITED

Abrash, Abigail, and Danny Kennedy. "Repressive Mining in West Papua." In *Moving Mountains: Communities Confront Mining and Globalisation*, edited by Geoff Evans, James Goodman and Nina Landsbury. Otford Press: Australia, Zed Books: UK, 2001. See also www.mpi.org.au/indon/eng_moving_mountains.html.

Agrawal, Arun. "Community in Conservation: Beyond Enchantment and Disenchantment." Discussion Paper. Gainesville, FL: Conservation and Development Forum, 1997.

Ahmed, Mubariq. "Stakeholder Statement Session Remarks." *NRM News* Vol. II, No. 2 (July 2000): 4.

Alcorn, Janis. "Huastec Non-Crop Resource Management: Implications for Prehistoric Rainforest Management." *Human Ecology* 9 (1981): 395–417.

Alcorn, Janis, and Antoinette G. Royo, eds. *Indigenous Social Movements and Ecological Resilience: Lessons from the Dayak of Indonesia*. Washington, DC: Biodiversity Support Program, 2000.

Altieri, M. A. "Rethinking Crop Genetic Resource Conservation: A View from the South." *Conservation Biology* 3, no. 1, (1989): 77–79.

Anderson, Benedict R. O'G, and Ruth McVey. "A Preliminary Analysis of the October 30, 1965 Coup in Indonesia." Ithaca: Cornell Modern Indonesia Project, 1971.

———. "The State and Minorities in Indonesia." In *Southeast Asian Tribal Groups and Ethnic Minorities: Prospects for the Eighties and Beyond*, edited by Ruth Taswell, 73–81. Cambridge, MA: Cultural Survival, 1987.

Bachriadi, Dianto. "Kekerasan dalam Persoalan Agraria dan Relevansi Tuntutan Dijalankannya Pembaruan Agraria di Indoensia Paska-Order Baru." Unpublished manuscript, Konsorsium Pembaruan Agraria, n.d.

Ball, John. *Indonesian Legal History 1602–1848*. Sydney: Oughtershaw, 1982.

Barber, Charles V. "The State, the Environment, and Development: The Genesis and Transformation of Social Forestry in New Order Indonesia." Ph.D. diss., University of California, Berkeley, 1989.

Barber, Charles V., and James Schweithelm, eds. *Trial by Fires: Forest Fires and Forestry Policy in Indonesia's Era of Crisis and Reform*. Washington, DC: World Resources Institute, 2000.

Barber, Charles V., Suraya Afiff, and Agus Purnomo. *Tiger by the Tail? Reorienting Biodiversity Conservation and Development in Indonesia*. Washington, DC: The World Resources Institute, 1995.

Barber, Charles V., and Kirk Talbott. "The Chainsaw and the Gun: The Role of the Military in Deforesting Indonesia." Paper presented at the Annual meeting of the Yale Chapter of the International Society of Tropical Foresters, "War and Tropical Forests: New Perspectives on Conservation in Areas of Armed Conflict." New Haven, CT, March 31–April 1, 2000.

Barr, Christopher M. "Bob Hasan, the Rise of Apkindo and the Shifting Dynamics of Control in Indonesia's Timber Sector." *Indonesia* 65 (1998): 1–36.

———. "Banking on Sustainability: Structural Adjustment and Forestry Reforms in Post-Suharto Indonesia." Bogor, Indonesia: Center for International Forestry Research (CIFOR), 2001.

Bediona Philipus, Iwan Tjitradjaja, Haris Palisuri, Arbab Paproeka, Gazali Hafid, Nasruddin, and Mansyur Latambaga. "Kasus Orang Moronene Buton Sulawesi Selatan, Menuju Pengelolaan Kawasan Lindung yang Lebih Manusiawi." Draft. P3AE-UI & ELSAM: Jakarta, 1999.

Bennagen, Ponciano, and Antoinette Royo, eds. *Mapping the Earth, Mapping Life*. Manila: Legal Rights and Natural Resources Center—Kasama sa Kalikasan, 2000.

Bennett, Chris P.A. "Village Governance and Decentralization of Natural Resource Management in Indonesia: Of Responsibility, Accountability and National Unity." Working Paper. Development and Planning Assistance, Sub-Project SP-81 Natural Resource Management Policy BAPPENAS-Hickling (CIDA), 2000a.

———. "Opposition to Decentralization: Sowing the Seeds of Future Conflict." Working Paper. Development and Planning Assistance, Sub-Project SP-81 Natural Resource Management Policy BAPPENAS-Hickling (CIDA), 2000b.

Black, Ian. "The *Lastposten*: Eastern Kalimantan and the Dutch in the Nineteenth and Early Twentieth Centuries." *Journal of South East Asian Studies* 16 (1985): 281–291.

Biodiversity Support Program (BSP). "Laporan Proses Lokakarya Penyususnan Kurikulum Penyelesaian Sengketa." BSP Kemala, Gadog, Bali, 27–30 January 1999.

Bowen, John. "On the Political Construction of Tradition: Gotong–Royong in Indonesia." *Journal of Asian Studies* XLV, no. 3, (1986): 545–561.

Bremen, Jan. *The Village on Java and the Early Colonial State*. Rotterdam: Erasmus University Press, 1982.

Bromley, Daniel W. "The Commons, Property, and Common Property Regimes." Paper presented at "Designing Sustainability on the Commons," the first annual conference of the International Association for the Study of Common Property, Duke University, NC, September 27–30, 1990.

Bromley, Daniel W. *Environment and Economy: Property Rights and Public Policy*. Cambridge, MA: Blackwell, 1991.

———. *Making the Commons Work: Theory, Practice, and Policy*. Oakland, CA: ICS Press, 1992.

————. "Property Regimes in Economic Development: Lessons and Policy Implications." In *Agriculture and the Environment: Perspectives on Rural Development,* edited by Ernst Lutz. Washington, DC: World Bank, 1998.

Bromley, Daniel W., and Espen Sjaastad. "Prejudices of Property Rights: Of Individualism, Specificity and Security in Property Regimes." *Development Policy Review,* Vol. 18, no. 4, (2000): 365–389.

Brown, D.W. *Addicted to Rent: Corporate and Spatial Distribution of Forest Resources in Indonesia.* Jakarta: DFID/IFMP, 1999.

Brush, Stephen, and Doreen Stabinsky, eds. *Valuing Local Knowledge: Indigenous People and Intellectual Property Rights.* Washington, DC: Island Press, 1996.

Burns, Peter. "The Myth of Adat." *Journal of Legal Pluralism and Informal Law* 28 (1989): 1–127.

Campbell, Jeffrey Y. "Forests for the People, Indigenous Communities, or Cooperatives? Plural Perspectives in the Policy Debate for Community Forestry in Indonesia." In *Which Way Forward? Forests People and Policy in Indonesia,* edited by Carol J.P. Colfer and Ida Aju Pradnja Resosudarmo. Washington, DC: Resources for the Future, 2001.

Casson, Anne. "Ethnic Violence in an Era of Regional Autonomy: A Background to the Bloodshed in Kotawaringan Timor." RMAP Occasional Paper, Resource Management in Asia-Pacific Project, RSPAS, ANU, 2001.

Chambers, Robert. "Rural Development: Whose Knowledge Counts?" *IDS Bulletin* 10, no. 2 (1979).

Chapin, Mac, and Bill Threlkeld. *Indigenous Landscapes: A Study in Ethnocartography.* Arlington, VA: Native Lands, 2001.

Colchester, Marcus, ed. *A Survey of Indigenous Land Tenure: A Report for the Land Tenure Service of the Food and Agriculture Organisation.* Rome: FAO, December 2001.

Colchester, Marcus. "Unity and Diversity: Indonesian Policy Towards Tribal Peoples." *The Ecologist* 16, no. 2-3 (1986): 89–98.

Colfer, Carol J.P., and Ida Aju Pradnja Resosudarmo, eds. *Which Way Forward? People, Forests and Policymaking in Indonesia.* Washington, DC: Resources for the Future, 2001.

Conklin, Harold C. *Hanunoo Agriculture: A Report on an Integral System of Shifting Cultivation in the Philippines.* Rome: Food and Agriculture Organization, 1957.

Coppel, Charles. *Indonesian Chinese in Crisis.* Kuala Lumpur: Oxford University Press, 1983.

Cribb, Robert. "The Politics of Environmental Protection In Indonesia." Working Paper. Centre of Southeast Asian Studies. Monash University, Clayton, Australia, 1988.

————. "Birds of Paradise and Environmental Politics in Colonial Indonesia, 1890–1931." In *Paper Landscapes: Explorations in the Environmental History of Indonesia,* edited by Peter Boomgaard, Freek Colombijn, and David Henley. Leiden: KITLV Press, 1997.

Crocombe, Ron. "An Approach to the Analysis of Land Tenure Systems." In *Land Tenure in the Pacific,* edited by Ron Crocombe. Melbourne: Oxford University Press, 1971.

de Foresta, H., A. Kusworo, G. Michon, and W.A. Djatmiko, eds. *Agroforest Khas Indonesia: Sebuah Sumbangan Masyarakat.* Bogor: ICRAF, 2001.

de Soto, Hernando. *The Mystery of Capital: Why Capitalism Triumphs in the West and Fails Everywhere Else.* New York: Basic Books, 2001.

Demsetz, Harold. "Toward a Theory of Property Rights." *American Economic Review* 57, no. 2 (1967): 347–359.

Departemen Kehutanan (DepHut). *Sejarah Kehutanan Indonesia.* Jakarta, 1986.

Derrida, Jacques. *Writing and Difference.* Chicago: University of Chicago Press, 1972.

————. *Of Grammatology.* Baltimore, MD: Johns Hopkins University Press, 1997.

Dietz, Tom. *Entitlements to Natural Resources, Contours of Political Environmental Geography.* Utrecht: International Books, 1996.

Dove, Michael R. "Theories of Swidden Agriculture and the Political Economy of Ignorance." *Agroforestry Systems* 1 (1983): 85–99.

———. "Government Perceptions of Traditional Social Forestry in Indonesia: The History, Causes, and Implications of State Policy on Swidden Agriculture." *Community Forestry: Socio-Economic Aspects.* Rome: Food and Agriculture Organization (1985): 147.

———. *Swidden Agriculture in Indonesia: Subsistence Strategies of The Kalimantan Kantu.* Berlin: Mouton, 1985.

———. "A Revisionist View of Tropical Deforestation and Development." *Environmental Conservation* 20, no. 1 (1993a): 17–24.

———. "Smallholder Rubber and Swidden Agriculture in Borneo: A Sustainable Adaptation to the Ecology and Economy of a Tropical Forest." *Economic Botany* 47, no. 2 (1993b): 136–147.

———. "So Far from Power, So Near the Forest: A Structural Analysis of Gain and Blame in Tropical Forest Development." In *Borneo in Transition: People, Forests, Conservation, and Development,* edited by Christine Padoch and Nancy Peluso. Kuala Lumpur: Oxford University Press, 1996.

———. "Living Rubber, Dead Land, and Persisting Systems in Borneo: Indigenous Representations of Sustainability." *Bijdragen* 154, no. 1 (1998): 1–35.

Dove, Michael R., and D.K. Kammen. "The Epistemology of Sustainable Resource Use: Managing Forest Products, Swiddens, and High-Yielding Variety Crops." *Human Organization* 56, no. 1 (1997): 91–101.

Dunn, J. *Timor: A People Betrayed.* Milton, Queensland: Jacaranda Press, 1983.

Echols, John M., and Hassan Shadily. *English-Indonesian Dictionary.* Ithaca: Cornell University Press, 1989.

Edmunds, David, and Eva Wollenburg. "A Strategic Approach to Multi-Stakeholder Negotiations." Unpublished manuscript, n.d.

Ellsworth, Lynn. *The Link Between Tenure Security and Community Livelihoods: A Review of the Theory, Evidence and Implications.* Washington, DC: Forest Trends, 2000.

Fauzi, Noer. "Keadilan Agraria Di Masa Transisi: Mewujudkan Pengakuan Atas Hak-Hak Agraria Penduduk Dan Pemulihan Kondisi Korban-Korban Sengketa Agraria." Paper presented at the National Commission on Human Rights' (KOMNAS HAM) Sixth Annual National Human Rights Seminar, Surabaya 21–24 November 2000, and at the Critical Studies of Decentralization Seminar. Badan Pelaksana Konsorsium Pembaruan Agraria/ Yayasan Pendidikan Rakyat dan Dewan Perwakilan Rakyat Kabupaten Donggala (Palu, 14–17 January 2000) (2000a).

Fauzi, Noer. "Budaya Menyangkal: Konsep dan Praktek Politik Hukum Agraria yang Menyangkal Kenyataan Hak-Hak Masyarakat." *Wacana* 6, no. 2 (2000b): 102–114.

Fay, Chip, and Martua Sirait. "Getting the Boundaries Right: Indonesia's Urgent Need to Redefine Its Forest Estate." Unpublished manuscript, n.d.

Fay, Chip, and Martua Sirait. "Reforming the Reformists: Challenges to Government Forestry Reform in Post-Suharto Indonesia." In *Which Way Forward? Forests People and Policy in Indonesia,* edited by Carol J.P. Colfer and Ida Aju Pradnja Resosudarmo. Washington, DC: Resources for the Future, 2001.

Fay, Chip, and Hubert de Foresta. "Progress Towards Increasing the Role Local People Play in Forestlands Management in Indonesia." Paper prepared for the Workshop on Participatory Natural Resource Management in Developing Countries, Mansfield College, Oxford, April 6-7, 1998.

Ferraro, Paul J. "Global Habitat Protection: Limitations of Development Interventions and a Role for Conservation Performance Payments." Department of Applied Economics and Management, Working Paper, Cornell University, Ithaca, NY (forthcoming in *Conservation Biology*), 2001.

Flavin, Christopher. "Rich Planet, Poor Planet." In *State of the World*, Lester Brown et al. Washington, DC: Worldwatch Institute, 2001.

Foucault, Michel. *The Archaeology of Knowledge.* New York: Pantheon Books, 1972.

Franke, R. "East Timor: Physical and Cultural Genocide." *Anthropological Humanism Quarterly* 6 (1981): 18–20.

Fried, Stephanie G. "Tropical Forest Forever? A Contextual Ecology of Bentian Rattan Agroforestry Systems." In *Peoples, Plants and Justice: The Politics of Nature Conservation,* edited by Charles Zerner. New York: Columbia University Press, 2000.

Furnivall, J.S. *Netherlands India: A Study of Plural Economy.* New York: Macmillan, 1944.

Geertz, Clifford. *Local Knowledge: Further Essays in Interpretive Anthropology.* New York: Basic Books, 1983.

Gellert, Paul. "A Brief History and Analysis of Indonesia's Forest Fire Crisis." *Indonesia* 65 (1998): 63–85.

Gollin, Karin, and James L. Kho. "The Linked Problems of Local Communities, Natural Resources, and Democracy: Approaches to a Philippine Program on Environmental Governance." Paper commissioned by the Ford Foundation Manila office. Manila, 2001.

Gullison, R.E., R.E. Rice, and A.G. Blundell. "'Marketing Species Conservation: Financial Incentives Can Be Found to Conserve a Species Threatened by Trade." *Nature* 404 (April 27, 2000): 923–924.

Harahap, H. "Pemanfaatan Hutan Dalam Menyejahterakan Masyarakat." Paper presented at the Seminar on Economic Democracy in the Forestry Sector. WALHI, Jakarta, 1991.

Hardin, Garrett. "The Tragedy of the Commons." *Science,* 162 (1968): 1243–1248.

Harwell, Emily. "Law and Culture in Resource Management: An Analysis of Local Systems for Resource Management in the Danau Sentarum Wildlife Reserve, West Kalimantan, Indonesia." Consultant's Report. Bogor: Wetlands International–Indonesia Programme, 1997.

———. "Remote Sensibilities: Discourses of Technology and the Making of Indonesia's Natural Disaster." *Development and Change* 31 (2000a): 307–340.

———. "The Un-Natural History of Culture: Ethnicity, Tradition and Territorial Conflicts in West Kalimantan, Indonesia, 1800–1997." Ph.D. Dissertation, Yale University School of Forestry and Environmental Studies. December 2000 (2000b).

Hefner, Robert. *Civil Islam.* Princeton, NJ: Princeton University Press, 2000.

Hohfeld, Wesley N. "Fundamental Legal Conceptions As Applied In Judicial Reasoning I." *Yale Law Journal* 23 (1913): 16.

Hohfeld, Wesley N. "Fundamental Legal Conceptions As Applied in Judicial Reasoning II." *Yale Law Journal* 26 (1917): 710.

Holleman, J.F., ed. *"Van Vollenhoven on Indonesian Adat Law: Selections from 'Het Adatrecht van Nederlandsch-Indie.'"* The Hague: Martinus Nijhoff, 1981.

Holmes, D. *Deforestation in Indonesia: A Review of the Situation in Sumatra, Kalimantan, and Sulawesi.* Jakarta: The World Bank, 2000.

Hooker, M.B. *Legal Pluralism: An Introduction to Colonial and Neo-colonial Laws.* Oxford: Clarendon, 1975.

Hooker, M.B. *Adat Law in Modern Indonesia.* Kuala Lumpur: Oxford University Press, 1978.

Human Rights Watch (HRW). "Trouble in Irian Jaya." New York: HRW Report, Jul 6 1998.

———. "Why Aceh is Exploding." New York: HRW Report, Aug 27, 1999.

———. "Human Rights and Pro-Independence Actions in Papua, 1999–2000." New York: HRW Report, 2000.

———. "Violence and Political Impasse in Papua." New York: HRW Report, Jul 3, 2001.

———. "The War in Aceh." New York: HRW Report, August 2001.

International Labor Organization (ILO). "Employment Challenges of the Indonesian Economic Crisis." Jakarta, November 2000.

Irwin, Graham. *Nineteenth Century Borneo: A Study in Diplomatic Rivalry.* 's Gravenhage, The Netherlands: Nijhoff, 1955.

Koesnoe, Mohammad H. "Perkembangan Hukum Adat Setelah Perang Dunia II dalam Rangka Pembaharuan Hukum Nasional." Paper presented at the Simposium Sejarah Hukum, BPHN, 1976.

———. *Hukum Adat Sebagai Suatu Model Hukum.* Pengarang: Penerbit Mandar Maju, 1992.

Kusworo, A. *Pengusiran Penduduk Dari Kawasan Hutan di Lampung.* Watala-ICRAF-ORSTOM. Bogor: Pustaka Latin, 2000.

Lansing, Stephen J. *Priests and Programmers: Technologies of Power in the Engineered Landscape of Bali.* Princeton, NJ: Princeton University Press, 1991.

Leighton, Mark, and Nengah Wirawan. "Catastrophic Drought and Fire in Borneo Associated with the 1982–83 El Niño Southern Oscillations Event." In *Tropical Rainforests and the World Atmosphere,* edited by Gillian Prance. Washington, DC: American Association for the Advancement of Science, 1986.

Lev, Daniel. "Judicial Unification in Post Colonial Indonesia." *Indonesia* 16 (October 1973): 1–13.

———. "Colonial Law and the Genesis of the Indonesian State." *Indonesia* 40 (October 1985): 56–74.

Li, Tania M. "Images of Community: Discourse and Strategy in Property Relations." *Development and Change* 27 (1996).

———. "Comprising Power: Development, Culture, and Rule in Indonesia." *Cultural Anthropology* 14(3) (1999): 295–323.

———. "Articulating Indigenous Identity in Indonesia: Resource Politics and the Tribal Slot." *Comparative Studies of History and Society.* Forthcoming.

Liew, Soo Chin, Oo Kaw Lim, Leong Keong Kwoh, and Hock Lim. "A Study of the 1997 Forest Fires in South East Asia using SPOT Quicklook Mosaics." Paper presented at the 1998

International Geoscience and Remote Sensing Symposium. Seattle, July 1998.

Lindblad, J. Thomas. *Between the Dayak and the Dutch: The Economic History of Southeast Kalimantan, 1880–1942.* Dordrect, Netherlands: Foris, 1988.

Lowe, Celia. "Global Markets, Local Injustice in the Southeast Asian Seas: The Live Fish Trade and Local Fishers in the Togean Islands of Sulawesi." In *People, Plants and Justice: The Politics of Nature Conservation,* edited by Charles Zerner, 234–258. New York: Columbia University Press, 2000.

Lowry, R. *The Armed Forces of Indonesia.* St. Leonards, Australia: Allen and Unwin, 1996.

Lynch, Owen J. "Indigenous Rights in Insular Southeast Asia." In *Southeast Asian Tribal Groups and Ethnic Minorities: Prospects for the Eighties and Beyond,* edited by Ruth Taswell, 27–45. Cambridge, MA: Cultural Survival, 1987.

———. "Whither the People? Demographic, Tenurial and Agricultural Aspects of the Tropical Forestry Action Plan." Washington, DC: World Resources Institute, 1990.

———. "Colonial Legacies in a Fragile Republic: A History of Philippine Land Law and State Formation with Emphasis on the Early U.S. Regime (1898–1913)." Doctor of Laws dissertation, Yale University, 1992.

———. "Promoting Legal Recognition of Community-Based Property Rights, Including the Commons: Some Theoretical Considerations." Paper presented at the Symposium of the International Association for the Study of Common Property and the Workshop in Political Theory and Policy Analysis, Indiana University, Bloomington, Indiana, June 7, 1999.

Lynch, Owen J., and Kirk Talbott. *Balancing Acts: Community-Based Forest Management and National Law in Asia and the Pacific.* Washington, DC: World Resources Institute, 1995.

Lynch, Owen J., and Ted Bonpin, et al, eds. *Rural Filipinos' Contributions to Environmental Justice and Sustainable Development: Local*

Case Studies on Law and Community-Based Natural Resource Management. Washington, DC: Center for International Environmental Law and Tanggol Kalikasan, forthcoming 2002.

Mackie, J.A.C. "The Lessons Behind East Kalimantan's Forest Fires." *Borneo Research Bulletin* 16 (1984): 63–74.

———. *Konfrontasi: The Indonesia-Malaysia Dispute 1963–1966.* Kuala Lumpur: Oxford University Press, 1974.

Mahmudi Ismail, Nur. Minister of Forestry's keynote address for the Irian Jaya Provincial Forestry Policy Discussion Workshop: "Pentingnya Perumusan Kebijakan Sektor Kehutanan Secara Bersama Sebagai Langkah Menuju Hutanyang Berkelanjutan." Irian Jaya 17–18 February 2001. Available at: http://www.dephut.go.id/informasi/menteri/loka_irja_17180201.htm.

Maine, Henry. *Ancient Law.* New York: Hippocrene Books, 1987.

Mainhardt, Heike. "IMF Intervention in Indonesia: Undermining Macroeconomic Stability and Sustainable Development by Perpetuating Deforestation." Washington, DC: World Wildlife Fund, Macroeconomics for Sustainable Development Office, 2001.

Mamdami, Mahmood. *Citizen and Subject: Contemporary Africa and the Legacy of Late Colonialism.* Princeton, NJ: Princeton University Press, 1996.

Mangunsong, Farma. "Aplikasi Penilaian Ekonomi Sumber Daya Alam untuk Analisis Konversi Lahan." Skripsi, Jurusan Ekonomi dan Kajian Pembangunan, Universitas Indonesia, Depok, 2000.

Mawardi, Dedy. "Hutan Kemasyarakatan: Peluang dan Implikasi Bagi Pengembangan SHK." Paper presented at the Seminar Kebijakan Sistem Hutan Kemasyarakatan. Jakarta: WALHI, 28 October 1996.

Mayer J H. "Trees vs. Trees: Institutional Dynamics of Indigenous Agroforestry and Industrial Timber in West Kalimantan, Indonesia." City and Regional Planning in the Graduate Division. Berkeley: University of California: 376, 1996.

McCay, Bonnie J., and James M. Acheson, eds. *The Question of the Commons: The Culture and Ecology of Communal Resources.* Tucson, AZ: University of Arizona Press, 1990.

Mendelsohn, Robert. "Property Rights and Tropical Deforestation." *Oxford Economic Papers* 46, no. 5 (1994): 750–756.

Michon G., H. de Foresta, and A. Kusworo, *Complex Agroforests of Indonesia*. Bogor: ICRAF. Forthcoming.

Milton, Giles. *Nathaniel's Nutmeg*. New York: Penguin, 1999.

Mittermeier, Russell A., and Cristina Goettsch Mittermeier. *Megadiversity*. Mexico: Conservation International, CEMEX, 1997.

MoFEC, 2000. *Rencana Stratejik 2001–2005 [Strategic Plan 2001– 2005]*. Jakarta: Ministry of Forestry and Plantations, July 2000.

Momberg, Frank, Kristianus Atok, and Martua Sirait. *Drawing on Local Knowledge: A Community Mapping Training Manual*. Jakarta, Indonesia: The Ford Foundation, WWF Indonesia Program, and Yayasan Karya Sosial Pancur Kasih, 1996.

Moniaga, Sandra. "Toward Community-Based Forestry and Recognition of Adat Property Rights in the Outer Islands of Indonesia." In *Legal Frameworks for Forest Management in Asia: Case Studies of Community/State Relations*, edited by Jefferson Fox, 131–150. Occasional papers of the Program on Government, no. 16. Honolulu, HI: East-West Center, 1993.

Muhsi, Muayat Ali. "Community Forest System Management (SHK) in Indonesia." *Voices from the Forest*, no. 3, Newsletter of the NTFP Exchange Programme in Southeast Asia (August 2000). Available at: http://www.ntfp.org/voices/voices3/contents3.html.

Murphree, Marshall W. "Articulating Voices from the Commons: Interpretation, Translation and Facilitation," *The Common Property Resource Digest* 38 (June 1996).

Nasution, Adnan Buyung. *The Aspiration for a Constitutional Government in Indonesia: A Socio-Legal Study of the Indonesian Konstituante, 1956–1959*. Jakarta: Pustaka Sinar Harapan, 1992.

Natural Resource Management Program (NRMP). "Dasar Hukum dan Rekomendasi Para Pihak untuk Penerapan 'Co-Management' dan Desentralisasi Sistem Pembiayaan Taman Nasional

Bunaken." Report to the Minister of Forestry. Jakarta, 12 December 2000 (2000a).

―――. "Kelayakan Teknis: Dewan Pengelolaan Taman Nasional Bunaken Sulawesi Utara Sebagai Model Pengelolaan Para Pihak Kawasan Pelestarian Alam di Indonesia." Report to the Governor of Northern Sulawesi. Manado, September 2000 (2000b).

Okoth-Ogendo, H.W.O. "The Tragic African Commons: A Century of Expropriation, Suppression and Subversion." Keynote address at the African Public Interest Law and Community-Based Property Rights Workshop, Arusha, Tanzania, August 2000.

Osborne, R. *Indonesia's Secret War: The Guerrilla Struggle in Irian Jaya.* Sydney: Allen and Unwin, 1985.

Ostrom, Elinor. *Governing the Commons: The Evolution of Institutions for Collective Action.* Cambridge, U.K.: Cambridge University Press, 1991.

Padoch, Christine. *Migration and Its Alternatives among the Iban of Sarawak.* The Hague: Martinus Nijhoff, 1982.

Panayotou, Theodore. *The Economics of Environmental Degradation: Problems, Causes, and Responses.* Cambridge, MA: Harvard Institute for International Development, 1989.

Patay, M., and A. Saway. "Dampak Kegiatan Perusahaan HPH terhadap kondisi Biofisik, Sosio-ekonomi dan Sosio-budaya di Kabupaten Yapen Waropen Irian Jaya." Irian Jaya: Yayasan Pengembangan Masyarakat Desa Irian Jaya (YPMD–IRJA), 1993.

Peltzer, Karl J. "Swidden Cultivation in Southeast Asia: Historical, Economic and Ecological Perspectives." In *Farmers in the Forest: Economic Development of Marginal Agriculture in Northern Thailand,* edited by Peter Kunstadter, 271–286. Honolulu, HI: East–West Center.

Peluso, Nancy L. *Rich Forests, Poor People: Resource Control and Resistance in Java.* Berkeley: University of California Press, 1992.

―――. "Coercing Conservation: The Politics of State Resource Control." *Global Environmental Change* 4, no. 2 (1993): 199–217.

Peluso, Nancy L., and Emily Harwell. "Territory, Custom, and the Cultural Politics of Ethnic War in West Kalimantan, Indonesia." In *Violent Environments*, edited by Nancy Peluso and Michael Watts, 145–205. Ithaca: Cornell University Press, 2001.

Peluso, Nancy L., and Peter Vandergeest. "Genealogies of Forest Law and Customary Rights in Indonesia, Malaysia and Thailand." *Journal of Asian Studies* (Under Review), n.d.

Peters, Charles M., Alwyn H. Gentry, and Robert O. Mendelsohn. "Valuation of an Amazonian Rainforest." *Nature* 339 (29 June 1989): 655–656.

Poore, Duncan. *No Timber Without Trees: Sustainability in the Tropical Forest.* London: Earthscan Publications Ltd., 1989.

Potter, Lesley. "Indigenes and Colonisers: Dutch Forest Policy in South and East Borneo in 1900–1950." In *Changing Tropical Forests: Historical Perspectives on Challenges in Today's Asia Australasia and Oceania,* edited by John Dargavel, Kay Dixon and Noel Simple, 127–153. Canberra: Centre for Resource and Environmental Studies, Australian National University, 1988.

———. "Environmental and Social Aspects of Timber Exploitation in Kalimantan, 1967–1989." In *Indonesia: Resources, Ecology and Environment,* edited by J. Hardjono. Singapore, Oxford: Oxford University Press, 1991.

Potter, Lesley, and Justin Lee. "Tree Planting in Indonesia: Trends, Impacts and Directions." Center for International Forestry (CIFOR) Occasional Paper 18. Bogor: CIFOR, 1998.

Rahardjo, Diah. "Daftar Bagian dan Pasal dalam UU Kehutanan 41/1999 yang Berkaitan Posisi Masyarakat Setempat dan Masyarakat Hukum Adat." Unpublished draft, 1999.

Ramos Horta, J. *Funu: The Unfinished Saga of East Timor.* Trenton, NJ: Red Sea Press, 1987.

Read, Tory, and Lafcadio Cortesi. *Stories at the Forest Edge: The KEMALA Approach to Good Governance and Sustainable Future.* Washigton, DC: Biodiversity Support Program, 201.

Reid, Anthony. *Southeast Asia in the Age of Commerce 1450–1680.* (vol. I, II). New Haven: Yale University Press, 1993.

Reisman, Michael W., and Aaron M. Scheiber. *Jurisprudence: Understanding and Shaping Law.* New Haven: Yale University Press, 1987.

Rhee, Steve. "De Facto Decentralization During a Period of Transition in East Kalimantan." *Asian-Pacific Community Forestry* 13, no. 2 (2000).

Ricklefs, M.C. *A History of Modern Indonesia.* Bloomington: Indiana University Press, 1981.

Robinson, Geoffry. *The Dark Side of Paradise: Political Violence in Bali.* Ithaca: Cornell University Press, 1995.

Rose, Carol. *Property and Persuasion: Essays on the History, Theory and Rhetoric of Ownership.* Boulder: Westview Press, 1994.

Ross, Michael L. *Timber Booms and Institutional Breakdown in Southeast Asia.* Cambridge, U.K.: Cambridge University Press, 2001.

Runge, Ford C. "Common Property and Collective Action in Economic Development." *World Development* 14, no. 5 (1986): 623–635.

Ruwiastuti, Maria Rita. *'Sesat Pikir': Politik Hukum Agraria, Menggugat Alas Pengusaan Negara atas Hak-Hak Adat.* Yogyakarta: INSIST Press, 2000.

Safitri, Myrna A. *Desa, Institusi Lokal dan Pengelolaan Hutan: Refleksi Kebijakan dan Praktik.* Jakarta: Lembaga Studi dan Advokasi Masyarakat (ELSAM), 1999.

Sari, Agus P. "Environmental and Human Right Impacts of Trade Liberalization: A Case Study in Batam Island, Indonesia." Berkeley, CA: The Nautilus Institute for Security and Sustainable Development, March 1998.

Scotland, N., A. Fraser, and N. Jewell. "Roundwood Supply and Demand in the Forest Sector in Indonesia." Indonesia–U.K. Tropical Forest Management Programme, 1999.

Scott, James C. *Domination and the Arts of Resistance.* New Haven, CT: Yale University Press, 1990.

———. *The Moral Economy of the Peasant: Rebellion and Resistance in Southeast Asia.* New Haven, CT: Yale University Press, 1976.

————. *Seeing Like a State: How Certain Schemes to Improve the Human Condition Have Failed.* New Haven: Yale University Press, 1998.

Sirait, Martua. n.d. "Pengelolaan Hutan Bertumpu pada Masyarakat di Indonesia." Unpublished manuscript.

Sirait, Martua, Chip Fay and A. Kusworo. "Bagaimana Hak-Hak Masyarakat Hukum Adat Dalam Mengelola Sumber Daya Alam Diatur?" Paper presented at Forestry Roundtable Discussion, Wisma PKBI (20 Oct 1999) and at the Seminar Perencanaan Tata Ruang Secara Partisipatif (WATALA and BAPPENAS, Propinsi Lampung, 11 Oct 2000).

Smith, Joyotee and Sara Scherr. "Capturing the Value of Forest Carbon for Local Livelihoods." Unpublished manuscript, n.d.

Soepomo, R. *Kedudukan Hukum Adat Dikemudian Hari.* Jakarta: Penerbit Kebangsaan Pustaka Rakjat, 1951.

Sukarnoputri, Megawati. "Restoring Democracy, Justice and Order in Indonesia: An Agenda for Reform" (mimeo.), 1997.

Sumarlan, Yanuar. "Towards A Community-Based Resource Management From A State-Controlled One: Legal Overview and Possibilities." ICRAF-SEA Programme, unpublished report, 1998.

Sunderlin, W. D., and I. A. P. Resosudarmo. "Rate and Causes of Deforestation in Indonesia: Towards a Resolution of Ambiguities." Occasional Paper No. 9. Bogor: CIFOR, 1996.

Tadjudin, Djuhendi. "Hutan Kemasyarakatan: Anggur Privatisasi dalam Botol Kemasyarakatan." Paper presented at LATIN diskusi rutin, Bogor, August 1999.

Tapol (The Indonesia Human Rights Campaign). *West Papua: The Obliteration of a People.* London: Calverts, 1983.

Ter Haar Bzn. Beginselen en Stelsel van het Adatrecht [K.Ng.Soebakti Poesponoto (penterj. Asas-asas dan Susunan Hukum Adat)]. Jakarta: Pradya Paramita, Cetakan XI, 1994.

Thongcahi Winichakul. *Siam Mapped: A History of the Geobody of a Nation.* Honolulu, HI: University of Hawaii Press, 1988.

Thrupp, Lori Ann, Susanna Hecht, Owen Lynch, and John Browder. *The Diversity and Dynamics of Shifting Cultivation: Myths, Realities and Political Ecology of Changing Land Use in the Tropics.* Washington, DC: World Resources Institute, 1996.

Tim Kajian Tiga Lembaga (ELSAM, LRA Padang, YBH Bantaya). "Legal Opinion (Legal Critical Analysis) Terhadap UU No. 41 Kehutanan 1999." *Wacana* 6, no. 2 (2000): 85–101.

Titahelu, Ronald Z. "Marine and Coastal Resources and Community-Based Property Rights: Indonesian Experiences." Paper presented at Marine and Coastal Resources and Community-Based Property Rights: A Philippine Workshop, Anilao, Batangas, Philippines, 12–15 June 2001.

Tomich Thomas P., A.M. Fagi, H. de Foresta, G. Michon, D. Murdiyarso, F. Stolle, and M. van Noordwijk, eds. "Alternatives to Slash and Burn in Indonesia: Summary Report and Synthesis of Phase II." ASB-Indonesia Report, no. 8. Bogor: ASB and ICRAF-SE Asia, 1998.

Vandergeest, Peter, and Nancy Peluso. "Territorialization and State Power in Thailand." *Theory and Society* 24 (1995): 385–426.

Warren, Carol. *Adat and Dinas: Balinese Communities in the Indonesian State.* Kuala Lumpur: Oxford University Press, 1995.

WARSI, Kawasan Bukit Duabelas: Kondis dan Peruntukkan Bagi Ruang Hidup Orang Rimba (Resume Usulan Perluasan Cagar Biosfer Bukit Duabelas), Warung Informasi Konservasi, Jambi, May 1999.

Western, David, and R. Michael Wright. *Natural Connections: Perspectives in Community-Based Conservation.* Washington, DC: Island Press, 1994.

Wignyosoebroto, Soetandyo. *Dari Hukum Kolonial ke Hukum Nasional: Dinamika Sosio-Politik Perkembangan Hukum di Indonesia.* Jakarta: Rajawali Press, 1994.

———. "Masyarakat Adat di Tengah Perubahan dalam Roundtable Discussion Pemulihan Hak-hak Masyarakat Adat." Jakarta, 24 March 1999.

Winters, J.A. "Suharto's Indonesia: Prosperity and Freedom for the Few." *Current History* 94, no. 596 (1995): 420–424.

―――. "Criminal Debt." In *Reinventing the World Bank,* edited by Jonathan R. Pincus and Jeffrey A. Winters. Ithaca, NY: Cornell University Press, 2001.

Wollenberg, Eva, and Hariadi Kartodihardjo. "Devolution and Indonesia's New Basic Forestry Law." In *Which Way Forward? Forests People and Policy in Indonesia,* edited by Carol J.P. Colfer and Ida Aju Pradnja Resosudarmo. Washington, DC: Resources for the Future, 2001.

Wolters, O.W. *Early Indonesian Commerce: A Study of the Origins of Srivijaya.* Ithaca: Cornell University Press, 1967.

World Bank. *The World Bank Participation Sourcebook.* Washington, DC: The World Bank, 1996.

―――. *Indonesia in Crisis: A Macro-Economic Update.* Washington, DC: The World Bank, 1998.

―――. "Deforestation in Indonesia: A Preliminary View of the Situation in 1999." Draft Report. Washington, DC: The World Bank, 2000a.

―――. *The Challenges of World Bank Involvement in Forests: An Evaluation of Indonesia's Forests and World Bank Assistance.* Washington, DC: The World Bank, 2000b.

―――. *Indonesia: Environment and Natural Resource Management in a Time of Transition.* Washington, DC: The World Bank, 2001.

Wrangham, Rachel. "Policies towards Traditional Communities in Indonesia's Forests: An Analysis of Changing Discourses, 1960–1999." In *Which Way Forward? Forests, People and Policy in Indonesia,* edited by Carol J.P. Colfer and Ida Aju Pradnja Resosudarmo. Washington, DC: Resources for the Future, 2001.

WWF-WARSI, Menggugat PT. SML & PT. AS dalam Alam Sumatera dan Pembangunan Edisi III, Rengat, February 1999.

Yamin, Mohammad. "Naskah Persiapan UUD 1945 Jilid I." Jakarta: Yayasan Prapanca, 1959.

Zakaria, Yando R. *Abih Tandeh: Mayarakat Desa di Bawah Rezim Orde Baru.* Yogyakarta: INSIST Press, 2000.

Zakaria, Yando R., and Noer Fauzi. "Pembaruan desa dan agraria dalam konteks otonomi daerah." Paper presented at seminar on "Evaluation and Planning for Leadership Training for Regional Autonomy and Formation of District Administrations." Badan Pelaksana Konsorsium Pembaruan Agraria (BP-KPA). Jakarta, Wisma PKBI, April 9–11, 2001.

Zerner, Charles. "Community Rights, Customary Law, and the Law of Timber Concessions in Indonesia's Forests: Legal Opinions and Alternatives in Designing the Commons." Consultant's Report to FAO. (Forestry Studies Grant UTF/INS/065), 1990.

———. "Through a Green Lens: The Construction of Customary Environmental Law and Community in Indonesia's Maluku Islands." *Law and Society Review* 28, no. 5 (1994): 1081–1121.

Press citations:

"Audit Shock: Jakarta's missing billions." *Straits Times*, 18 July 2000.

"Defense Chief Vows to Crush Aceh rebels." *Media Indonesia*, 2 June 1999.

"Indonesia's Fires: Smoke as a Problem, Smoke as a Symptom." *Agroforestry Today* 10, no. 1, (January–March 1998): 4–7.

"Indonesia's Inferno Will Make Us All Sweat." *New Scientist*, October 4 1997.

"Indonesia's Papua Referendum was a Farce–Ex-UN Officials." *Associated Press*, 21 November 2001.

"Javanese Farmers Take Over Golf Courses." *International Market Insight Reports*, 21 October 1998.

"Minister Calls for Army to Deal with Separatist Groups." *Antara News Agency*, 12 March 2001.

"No Flags for Papua," *The Economist*, 14 October 2000.

"Now Aceh Takes a Beating: Are Indonesia's Security Forces Trying to Orchestrate Violence in Aceh?" *The Economist*, 11 March 2000.

"Oil Palm Plantations: Doing More Harm Than Good?" *Jakarta Post*, 6 February 2001.

"Police Declare 'War' on Irian Jaya Activists." *Straits Times*. 9 December 2000.

"Poor Invade Suharto Ranch in Battle against Starvation." *The Guardian*, 20 July 1998.

"The Push for Indigenous Rights." *Down to Earth* No. 36, 1998.

"Regional Autonomy Laws to be Revised." *Jakarta Post*, 29 August 2001.

"Rela Mati Demi Tanah Dayak." *Kalimantan Review*, no. 38 VII, (October 1998: 16-17).

Runyan, Curtis. "Indonesia's Discontent." *Worldwatch Magazine* 1998.

"Scorched Earth: Indonesia's Military Brings Chaos to East Timor." *Far Eastern Economic Review (FEER)*, 16 September 1999.

"The Soeharto Lobby," *The Progressive*, Eyal Press, May 1997.

APPENDIX 1

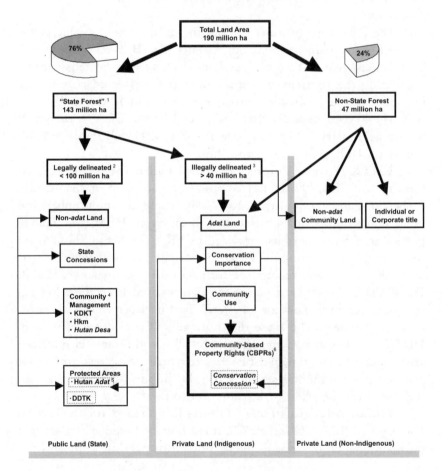

Possible Forest Tenure Arrangements

Note: Adapted in part from Sirait (n.d.).

Notes on Possible Forest Tenure Arrangements

1. Forest Classifications were done through the Consensus Forest Land Use Plan (TGHK), provided for in UUPK 5/1964; PP 33/1974 of Forest Planning, SK MenTan 680/1980, 837/1980, 683/1980, 681/1980 on Forest Planning Criteria; SK DirJenHut 85/1974 on Forest Delineation, revised by SK MenHut 634/1996, SK DirJen INTAG (Forest Inventory and Designation) 724/ 1994, and SK DirJen INTAG 82/1998 on Guidelines for Forest Delineation. Also, although the state claims 143 m ha as "State Forest," by its own admission only ~ 90 m ha of this area is still actually forested. See chapter 5 for more discussion

2. There were irregularities at both the central level, in which 68% of the forest classification announcements (BATB) were never signed by the Minister, and at the field level, in which a variety of requirements stipulating the participation and consent of affected community members in the delineation process were routinely violated.

3. The Revised Basic Forestry Law (UU41/1999, Article 1, paragraph 6) and a Ministry of Forestry Decree (SK 32/1999) disallow State Forest on land with prior ownership.

4. **KDTK** (Special Purpose Areas, provided for in the revised forestry law UU41/99) is derived from the precedent in Krui damar forests in Lampung Sumatra (SK 47/98). These are (non-timber) use rights only, contingent on maintained forest cover. **HkM** (Community Forest) are 25-year permits (provided by SK 677/98 and SK 685/99) for community logging. They are use rights, not management or ownership rights and require the formation of a cooperative. **Hutan Desa** (Village Forest) is a village use right derived from these logging co-ops, which may allow for long-term local management of resources other than timber. These use rights are all still considered state land. **DDTK** (Conservation Communities) are villages in or around protected areas that received special rewards for protecting resources that provide environmental services for the public (including carbon sequestration, flooding or erosion control).

5. **Hutan Adat** (Customary Forest) is provided for in Revised Forestry Law (UU41/99, article 67). It is a restricted use right (contingent on maintenance of forest cover), not an ownership right and the

area covered is still considered state land. See Chapter 5 for more discussion.

6. Community Based Property Rights (**CBPRs**). See Chapter One. Legal recognition of private CBPRs is provided for by various Indonesian laws, including a Ministerial Decision by the National Agrarian Board (PerMen BPN 5/99) and a Government Regulation (PP 24/97). They are non-transferable rights but have no other restrictions on use.

7. "**Conservation Concessions**" are zones within community territory, which remain under community title, but because of their conservation importance are granted privately funded easements in exchange for community protection from development or logging. Local NTFP or subsistence timber uses are still permitted under this agreement, but clearing for agriculture is not. (Conservation Concession agreements may also be feasible to protect state logging concessions or privately held land.)

APPENDIX 2. POSSIBLE ARRANGEMENTS FOR COMMUNITY RIGHTS IN NATURAL RESOURCE MANAGEMENT

	Supporting Legislation	Community Type	Resource Type	Rights	Public or Private	Complexity of Recognition Process	Comments
CBPR	PerMen BPN 5/1999	Adat (under current legislation, but could be expanded)	Multiple (marine, forest, fallow, etc)	Non-transferable Ownership	Private, secure	High	Current legislation is weak—Ministerial Decree not binding enough under decentralization
Customary Forest (Hutan Adat)	UU41.1999 RPP Hutan Adat	Adat	Forest	Restricted Use	Public, insecure	High	Requires state criteria, revocable
Special Use Areas (KDTK)	SK 47/1998	Non-adat, Adat	Managed Forest	Restricted Use	Public, insecure	Med	
Community Forest (HkM)	SK 32, 677	Non-Adat, Adat	Forest	35 year renewable use right for resource enterprise only	Public, insecure	Med	Requires formation of co-op
Community Concession or Environmental Service Reward	None yet, but could be based on BPN 5, SK 47	Non adat, Adat	Any of Conservation importance (marine or terrestrial)	Restricted Use Zone within Ownership Rights (Easement)	Private, ownership secure	Med	Incentive to conserve resources; benefits revocable if agreement is violated.

Note: Adapted in part from Sirait et al. (2000).

APPENDIX 3

CHALLENGES OF ADAT RECOGNITION: NOTES FROM THE FIELD[1]

During the Congress of Adat Leaders in Indonesia (AMAN) in 1999, a new demand emerged: "If the State will not recognize *adat* communities, the *adat* communities will not recognize the state!" This provocative statement received much attention in the media and government and has grown to be a battle cry of the indigenous peoples' movement in Indonesia. Yet, since the Congress AMAN leaders have struggled to address the enormous needs of adat communities throughout the archipelago and to develop appropriate methods of support that accommodate the immense variety of adat settings and experiences.

In March 2001, AMAN, ICRAF, and the Forest Peoples Program carried out an initial series of eight workshops within *adat* communities in Sulawesi, East Kalimantan and West Kalimantan. This team worked with local *adat* leaders and communities in selected areas to think through the basic questions that emerge from their fundamental demand for State recognition of their rights. The questions that emerged were:

1. What type or form of recognition do you seek, at what level, and what do you envision the process to be?
2. What type of rights is being demanded? For example, what type of land titles?
3. What institution and/or individual(s) represent you in dealings with the world outside your *adat* territory?
4. What level of self-governance and autonomy is being demanded, and how will the *adat* autonomous area relate to the Indonesian state?

As expected, there was significant variation in the way working groups approached these questions. Yet of the approximate 35 groups involved in these discussions, none envisioned gaining autonomy for an area larger than their main *adat* political unit, which was, without exception, smaller than an average district (*Kabupaten*).

After each working group reported back, FPP, ICRAF and AMAN recorded the responses and the team facilitated a discussion on each question, using examples from other countries to stimulate ideas and analysis. Most experiences that were shared centered on examples where indigenous communities in other parts of the world have faced complicated problems of governance, (when traditional structure could no longer handle the demands and pressures from the outside the community), and/or have lost their lands because the rights were transferable and were subsequently sold. Of all the issues that were raised in the workshops, these were the ones of greatest interest to participants.

The following are three of the team's primary observations of the workshop:

1. Leaders with close physical and political attachments to their communities have a clearer vision of their constituents' definitions of *adat* rights and their goals for recognition than do those leaders more loosely associated with their communities.

2. The communities consulted for the workshop have not yet reflected on how they hope to gain recognition of their *adat* rights. Nearly without exception, the workshop was the first time participants attempted to articulate these goals. This points to the urgent need for a systematic program of information dissemination and consultation, in which communities are presented with possible alternatives, and assisted in developing goals and strategies. In short, it appears necessary to move beyond emotional slogans and the short-term "fire fighting" approach, toward strengthening strategic legal tools and goals (aimed at the national, provincial, and district levels), as well as an ability to build local constituencies and respond to the wide variety of community demands and needs.

3. *Adat* communities that participated in these workshops, without exception, recognized the need for *adat* to continue to evolve towards a greater emphasis on equity, particularly in terms of access to natural resources and greater respect for women. This emphasized the need for *adat* communities to better articulate that *adat* governance, like Western democracies, is dynamic, ever evolving.

Finally, one of the greatest challenges that *adat* communities, AMAN, and supporting NGOs face is to engage effectively and assert pressure in the legal and policy development processes that are emerging and described in this report. It is now government policy to respect *adat* rights, and without effective engagement from the communities as primary stakeholders, badly designed policies and laws may result and be worse than the status quo.

Notes

1. From Fay and Sirait, personal fieldnotes.